The Welsh Marilyns

A Marilyn is a hill in the British Isles that has at leas height - 159 of the UK's Marilyns sit within the fabul beautiful coastlines and quaint, rural villages. The n often been dismissed for the more famous Lake District and Peak District National Parks, this being said you will struggle to find more breath-taking views than from the peaks of the mountains in Wales. With three national parks, each with their own unique geographical features, enjoy the views of lowland valleys and the wonderful welsh coastline - which can be seen from the peaks of some of the Marilyns!

This log book contains all 159 Welsh Marilyns. Most lie within the two largest national parks of Snowdonia and Brecon Beacons, however a good selection of the others are scattered across the country, overlooking rugged landscapes, rivers, coastlines and even small islands!

So get your hiking boots on and hit the great Welsh hills and log your adventures as you go!!!

Using the book is easy, use the map page to plan your next adventure and scan the QR code using your smartphone on the page of the Marilyn(s) you are planning on bagging - this will open a map of the peak.
You can zoom in and out accordingly to plan your route. Each Marylin has an OS grid reference which you can enter into your GPS system to follow on the day.

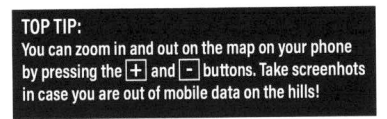

TOP TIP:
You can zoom in and out on the map on your phone by pressing the [+] and [-] buttons. Take screenhots in case you are out of mobile data on the hills!

Make sure when you have bagged your Marilyns, tick them off on the contents page and fill in the tick on your log page after you have filled in your adventure details!

Enjoy your hiking!

Hiking can be dangerous without proper planning and preparation, this activity is taken at your own risk. Please equip yourself with necessary supplies and equipment for your adventure and notify friends or relatives in advance of your hike of your planned route. All Marilyn information and locations correct at time of printing.

#	Name	Height
1.	Aberedw Hill	450.9m
2.	Allt y Main	356m
3.	Allt yr Esgair	392.6m
4.	Allt-Fawr [Allt Fawr]	698m
5.	Aran Fawddwy	905m
6.	Arenig Fach	689m
7.	Arenig Fawr	854m
8.	Banc Llechwedd-mawr	560m
9.	Beacon Hill	547m
10.	Black Mountain	703.6m
11.	Brandy Hill	206m
12.	Bryn Amlwg	488m
13.	Bryn Arw	385m
14.	Bryn y Fan	482m
15.	Cadair Berwyn	832m
16.	Cadair Idris - Penygadair	892.7m
17.	Caeliber Isaf	353.5m
18.	Carn Fadryn	371m
19.	Carn Gafallt	466m
20.	Carnedd Llewelyn	1064m
21.	Carnedd Wen	523m
22.	Carnedd y Filiast	669m
23.	Carneddau	445m
24.	Carneddol	235.9m
25.	Cefn Cenarth	460m
26.	Cefn Eglwysilan	382m
27.	Cefn yr Ystrad	617.3m
28.	Coety Mountain (Mynydd Coety)	578m
29.	Corndon Hill	513.6m
30.	Craig Cwm Silyn	734m
31.	Craig Goch (Mynydd Cwmcelli)	468.3m
32.	Craig y Castell	321m
33.	Craig y Llyn	600m
34.	Craig yr Allt	273m
35.	Creigiau Gleision	678m
36.	Crugiau Merched	462m
37.	Cyrn-y-Brain	564.6m
38.	Disgwylfa Fawr	507m
39.	Drosgol	550m
40.	Drygarn Fawr	645m
41.	Elidir Fawr	924m
42.	Esgair Ddu	464m
43.	Esgeiriau Gwynion (Foel Rhudd)	671m
44.	Fan Brycheiniog - Twr y Fan Foel	802.5m
45.	Fan Fawr	734m
46.	Fan Gyhirych	725m
47.	Fan Nedd	663m
48.	Ffridd Cocyn	312.8m
49.	Foel Cae'rberllan	380m
50.	Foel Cedig	667.4m
51.	Foel Cwmcerwyn	536m
52.	Foel Fenlli	510.9m
53.	Foel Fynyddau	370m
54.	Foel Goch	611m
55.	Foel Offrwm	405m
56.	Frenni Fawr	395m
57.	Gamallt	288m
58.	Garn Boduan	279m
59.	Garreg Lwyd	498.1m
60.	Garreg-hir	484.9m
61.	Garth Hill	307m
62.	Glasgwm	779m
63.	Glyder Fawr	1000.9m
64.	Graig Syfyrddin (Edmund's Tump)	423m
65.	Great Orme	207.1m
66.	Great Rhos	660m
67.	Gwastedyn Hill	477m
68.	Gwaunceste Hill	542m
69.	Gyrn Ddu	522.1m
70.	Gyrn Moelfre	523m
71.	Hafod Ithel	361m
72.	Hirfynydd	481m
73.	Holyhead Mountain	220m
74.	Hope Mountain	330m
75.	Llan Ddu Fawr (Waun Claerddu)	594m
76.	Long Mountain	408m
77.	Maesglase	678.5m
78.	Manod Mawr	661m
79.	Moel Cynghorion	674m
80.	Moel Eilio	726m
81.	Moel Famau	554.8m
82.	Moel Gyw	467m
83.	Moel Hebog	783m
84.	Moel Llyfnant	751m
85.	Moel Siabod	872.2m
86.	Moel y Dyniewyd	382.4m
87.	Moel y Gamelin	576.9m
88.	Moel y Golfa	403.2m
89.	Moel Ysgyfarnogod	623m
90.	Moel-ddu	553m
91.	Moel-y-gest	263m
92.	Moelfre	589m
93.	Moelwyn Mawr	770m
94.	Mwdwl-eithin	532m
95.	Myarth	292m
96.	Mynydd Allt-y-grug	338.7m
97.	Mynydd Anelog	191.4m
98.	Mynydd Bodafon (Yr Arwydd)	177.6m
99.	Mynydd Carn-y-cefn	550m
100.	Mynydd Carningli	346m
101.	Mynydd Cynros	329m
102.	Mynydd Dinas	258.1m
103.	Mynydd Drumau	272m
104.	Mynydd Enlli	167.9m
105.	Mynydd Epynt (Mynydd Eppynt)	475.5m
106.	Mynydd Llangorse	515m
107.	Mynydd Llangyndeyrn	263m
108.	Mynydd Machen	363.2m
109.	Mynydd Marchywel	418m
110.	Mynydd Mawr	698m
111.	Mynydd Nodol	539m
112.	Mynydd Rhiw	304m
113.	Mynydd Rhyd Ddu	389m
114.	Mynydd Sylen	284m
115.	Mynydd Troed	609m
116.	Mynydd Twyn-glas	472m
117.	Mynydd Uchaf	357m
118.	Mynydd y Betws	373.1m
119.	Mynydd y Cwm (Coed Cwm)	304.8m
120.	Mynydd y Glyn	377m
121.	Mynydd y Lan	381.3m
122.	Mynydd-y-briw	341m
123.	Pegwn Mawr	586m
124.	Pen Llithrig y Wrach	798.6m
125.	Pen y Fan	886m
126.	Pen y Garn	611m
127.	Pen y Garn-goch	487m
128.	Pen-crug-melyn	326m
129.	Penycloddiau	439.5m
130.	Pumlumon Fawr (Plynlimon)	752m
131.	Rhialgwm	540m
132.	Rhinog Fawr	720m
133.	Rhiw Gwraidd	442m
134.	Rhinog Fach	712m
135.	Rhobell Fawr	734m
136.	Rhos Ymryson	327m
137.	Snowdon - Yr Wyddfa	1085m
138.	Stingwern Hill	358m
139.	Sugar Loaf	596m
140.	Tal y Fan	610m
141.	Tarren y Gesail	667m
142.	Tarrenhendre	634m
143.	The Begwns	415m
144.	Tor y Foel	551m
145.	Trichrug	415m
146.	Trum y Ddysgl	709m
147.	Tryfan	917.5m
148.	Upper Park	352m
149.	Waun Fach	811m
150.	Waun Rydd	769.2m
151.	Wentwood	309.1m
152.	Y Garn	629m
153.	Y Garn	947m
154.	Y Golfa	341.4m
155.	Y Llethr	756m
156.	Y Lliwedd	898m
157.	Yr Aran	747.2m
158.	Yr Eifl	560.7m
159.	Ysgyryd Fawr	486m

Marilyn Map
At a glance....

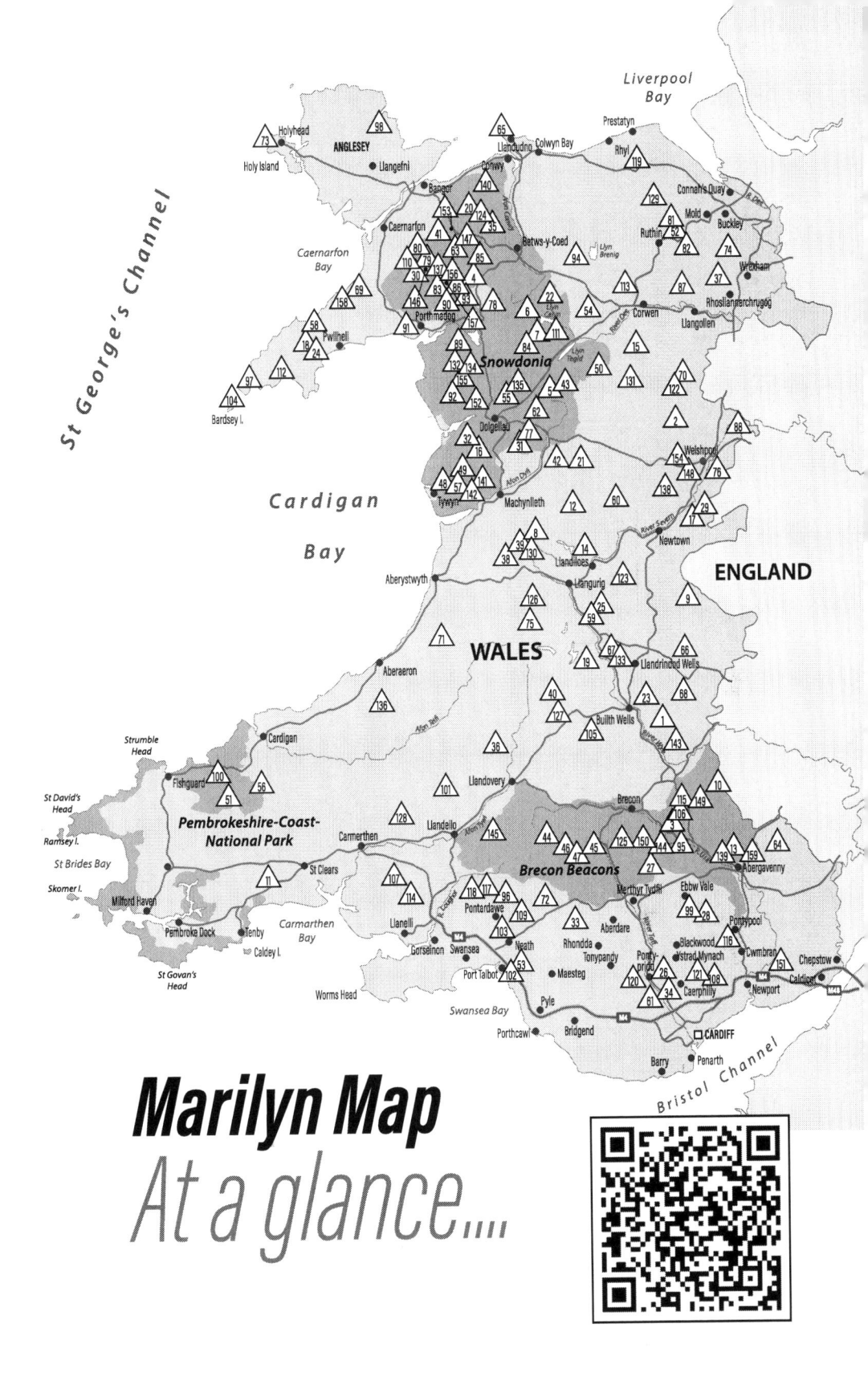

Fell Finder - Alphabetical Order

✓	Name	#
○	Aberedw Hill	1
○	Allt y Main	2
○	Allt yr Esgair	3
○	Allt-Fawr [Allt Fawr]	4
○	Aran Fawddwy	5
○	Arenig Fach	6
○	Arenig Fawr	7
○	Banc Llechwedd-mawr	8
○	Beacon Hill	9
○	Black Mountain	10
○	Brandy Hill	11
○	Bryn Amlwg	12
○	Bryn Arw	13
○	Bryn y Fan	14
○	Cadair Berwyn	15
○	Cadair Idris - Penygadair	16
○	Caeliber Isaf	17
○	Carn Fadryn	18
○	Carn Gafallt	19
○	Carnedd Llewelyn	20
○	Carnedd Wen	21
○	Carnedd y Filiast	22
○	Carneddau	23
○	Carneddol	24
○	Cefn Cenarth	25
○	Cefn Eglwysilan	26
○	Cefn yr Ystrad	27
○	Coety Mountain (Mynydd Coety)	28
○	Corndon Hill	29
○	Craig Cwm Silyn	30
○	Craig Goch (Mynydd Cwmcelli)	31
○	Craig y Castell	32
○	Craig y Llyn	33
○	Craig yr Allt	34
○	Creigiau Gleision	35
○	Crugiau Merched	36
○	Cyrn-y-Brain	37
○	Disgwylfa Fawr	38
○	Drosgol	39
○	Drygarn Fawr	40

✓	Name	#
○	Elidir Fawr	41
○	Esgair Ddu	42
○	Esgeiriau Gwynion (Foel Rhudd)	43
○	Fan Brycheiniog - Twr y Fan Foel	44
○	Fan Fawr	45
○	Fan Gyhirych	46
○	Fan Nedd	47
○	Ffridd Cocyn	48
○	Foel Cae'rberllan	49
○	Foel Cedig	50
○	Foel Cwmcerwyn	51
○	Foel Fenlli	52
○	Foel Fynyddau	53
○	Foel Goch	54
○	Foel Offrwm	55
○	Frenni Fawr	56
○	Gamallt	57
○	Garn Boduan	58
○	Garreg Lwyd	59
○	Garreg-hir	60
○	Garth Hill	61
○	Glasgwm	62
○	Glyder Fawr	63
○	Graig Syfyrddin (Edmund's Tump)	64
○	Great Orme	65
○	Great Rhos	66
○	Gwastedyn Hill	67
○	Gwaunceste Hill	68
○	Gyrn Ddu	69
○	Gyrn Moelfre	70
○	Hafod Ithel	71
○	Hirfynydd	72
○	Holyhead Mountain	73
○	Hope Mountain	74
○	Llan Ddu Fawr (Waun Claerddu)	75
○	Long Mountain	76
○	Maesglase	77
○	Manod Mawr	78
○	Moel Cynghorion	79
○	Moel Eilio	80

Fell Finder - Alphabetical Order

✓	Name	#
○	Moel Famau	81
○	Moel Gyw	82
○	Moel Hebog	83
○	Moel Llyfnant	84
○	Moel Siabod	85
○	Moel y Dyniewyd	86
○	Moel y Gamelin	87
○	Moel y Golfa	88
○	Moel Ysgyfarnogod	89
○	Moel-ddu	90
○	Moel-y-gest	91
○	Moelfre	92
○	Moelwyn Mawr	93
○	Mwdwl-eithin	94
○	Myarth	95
○	Mynydd Allt-y-grug	96
○	Mynydd Anelog	97
○	Mynydd Bodafon (Yr Arwydd)	98
○	Mynydd Carn-y-cefn	99
○	Mynydd Carningli	100
○	Mynydd Cynros	101
○	Mynydd Dinas	102
○	Mynydd Drumau	103
○	Mynydd Enlli	104
○	Mynydd Epynt (Mynydd Eppynt)	105
○	Mynydd Llangorse	106
○	Mynydd Llangyndeyrn	107
○	Mynydd Machen	108
○	Mynydd Marchywel	109
○	Mynydd Mawr	110
○	Mynydd Nodol	111
○	Mynydd Rhiw	112
○	Mynydd Rhyd Ddu	113
○	Mynydd Sylen	114
○	Mynydd Troed	115
○	Mynydd Twyn-glas	116
○	Mynydd Uchaf	117
○	Mynydd y Betws	118
○	Mynydd y Cwm (Coed Cwm)	119
○	Mynydd y Glyn	120

✓	Name	#
○	Mynydd y Lan	121
○	Mynydd-y-briw	122
○	Pegwn Mawr	123
○	Pen Llithrig y Wrach	124
○	Pen y Fan	125
○	Pen y Garn	126
○	Pen y Garn-goch	127
○	Pen-crug-melyn	128
○	Penycloddiau	129
○	Pumlumon Fawr (Plynlimon)	130
○	Rhialgwm	131
○	Rhinog Fawr	132
○	Rhiw Gwraidd	133
○	Rhinog Fach	134
○	Rhobell Fawr	135
○	Rhos Ymryson	136
○	Snowdon - Yr Wyddfa	137
○	Stingwern Hill	138
○	Sugar Loaf	139
○	Tal y Fan	140
○	Tarren y Gesail	141
○	Tarrenhendre	142
○	The Begwns	143
○	Tor y Foel	144
○	Trichrug	145
○	Trum y Ddysgl	146
○	Tryfan	147
○	Upper Park	148
○	Waun Fach	149
○	Waun Rydd	150
○	Wentwood	151
○	Y Garn	152
○	Y Garn	153
○	Y Golfa	154
○	Y Llethr	155
○	Y Lliwedd	156
○	Yr Aran	157
○	Yr Eifl	158
○	Ysgyryd Fawr	159

Fell Finder - Height Ascending

Height	Name	#	Height	Name	#
167.9m	Mynydd Enlli	104	377m	Mynydd y Glyn	120
177.6m	Mynydd Bodafon (Yr Arwydd)	98	380m	Foel Cae'rberllan	49
191.4m	Mynydd Anelog	97	381.3m	Mynydd y Lan	121
206m	Brandy Hill	11	382m	Cefn Eglwysilan	26
207.1m	Great Orme	66	382.4m	Moel y Dyniewyd	86
220m	Holyhead Mountain	73	385m	Bryn Arw	13
235.9m	Carneddol	24	389m	Mynydd Rhyd Ddu	113
258.1m	Mynydd Dinas	102	392.6m	Allt yr Esgair	3
263m	Moel-y-gest	91	395m	Frenni Fawr	56
263m	Mynydd Llangyndeyrn	107	403.2m	Moel y Golfa	88
272m	Mynydd Drumau	103	405m	Foel Offrwm	55
273m	Craig yr Allt	34	408m	Long Mountain	76
279m	Garn Boduan	58	415m	The Begwns	143
284m	Mynydd Sylen	114	415m	Trichrug	145
288m	Gamallt	57	418m	Mynydd Marchywel	109
292m	Myarth	95	423m	Graig Syfyrddin (Edmund's Tump)	64
304m	Mynydd Rhiw	112	439.5m	Penycloddiau	129
304.8m	Mynydd y Cwm (Coed Cwm)	119	442m	Rhiw Gwraidd	133
307m	Garth Hill	61	445m	Carneddau	23
309.1m	Wentwood	151	450.9m	Aberedw Hill	1
312.8m	Ffridd Cocyn	48	460m	Cefn Cenarth	25
321m	Craig y Castell	32	462m	Crugiau Merched	36
326m	Pen-crug-melyn	128	464m	Esgair Ddu	42
327m	Rhos Ymryson	136	466m	Carn Gafallt	19
329m	Mynydd Cynros	101	467m	Moel Gyw	82
330m	Hope Mountain	74	468.3m	Craig Goch (Mynydd Cwmcelli)	31
338.7m	Mynydd Allt-y-grug	96	472m	Mynydd Twyn-glas	116
341m	Mynydd-y-briw	122	475.5m	Mynydd Epynt (Mynydd Eppynt)	108
341.4m	Y Golfa	154	477m	Gwastedyn Hill	67
346m	Mynydd Carningli	100	481m	Hirfynydd	72
352m	Upper Park	148	482m	Bryn y Fan	14
353.5m	Caeliber Isaf	17	484.9m	Garreg-hir	60
356m	Allt y Main	2	486m	Ysgyryd Fawr	153
357m	Mynydd Uchaf	117	487m	Pen y Garn-goch	127
358m	Stingwern Hill	138	488m	Bryn Amlwg	12
361m	Hafod Ithel	71	498.1m	Garreg Lwyd	59
363.2m	Mynydd Machen	108	507m	Disgwylfa Fawr	38
370m	Foel Fynyddau	53	510.9m	Foel Fenlli	52
371m	Carn Fadryn	18	513.6m	Corndon Hill	29
373.1m	Mynydd y Betws	118	515m	Mynydd Llangorse	106

Fell Finder - Height Ascending

Height	Name	#
522.1m	Gyrn Ddu	69
523m	Carnedd Wen	21
523m	Gyrn Moelfre	70
532m	Mwdwl-eithin	94
536m	Foel Cwmcerwyn	5
539m	Mynydd Nodol	111
540m	Rhialgwm	131
542m	Gwaunceste Hill	68
547m	Beacon Hill	9
550m	Drosgol	39
550m	Mynydd Carn-y-cefn	99
551m	Tor y Foel	144
553m	Moel-ddu	90
554.8m	Moel Famau	81
560m	Banc Llechwedd-mawr	8
560.7m	Yr Eifl	58
564.6m	Cyrn-y-Brain	37
576.9m	Moel y Gamelin	87
578m	Coety Mountain (Mynydd Coety)	28
586m	Pegwn Mawr	123
589m	Moelfre	92
594m	Llan Ddu Fawr (Waun Claerddu)	75
596m	Sugar Loaf	139
600m	Craig y Llyn	33
609m	Mynydd Troed	115
610m	Tal y Fan	140
611m	Foel Goch	54
611m	Pen y Garn	126
617.3m	Cefn yr Ystrad	27
623m	Moel Ysgyfarnogod	89
629m	Y Garn	152
634m	Tarrenhendre	142
645m	Drygarn Fawr	40
660m	Great Rhos	66
661m	Manod Mawr	78
663m	Fan Nedd	47
667m	Tarren y Gesail	141
667.4m	Foel Cedig	50
669m	Carnedd y Filiast	22
671m	Esgeiriau Gwynion (Foel Rhudd)	43

Height	Name	#
674m	Moel Cynghorion	79
678m	Creigiau Gleision	35
678.5m	Maesglase	77
689m	Arenig Fach	6
698m	Allt-Fawr [Allt Fawr]	4
698m	Mynydd Mawr	110
703.6m	Black Mountain	10
709m	Trum y Ddysgl	146
712m	Rhinog Fach	134
720m	Rhinog Fawr	132
725m	Fan Gyhirych	46
726m	Moel Eilio	80
734m	Craig Cwm Silyn	30
734m	Fan Fawr	45
734m	Rhobell Fawr	135
747.2m	Yr Aran	157
751m	Moel Llyfnant	84
752m	Pumlumon Fawr (Plynlimon)	130
756m	Y Llethr	155
769.2m	Waun Rydd	150
770m	Moelwyn Mawr	93
779m	Glasgwm	62
783m	Moel Hebog	83
798.6m	Pen Llithrig y Wrach	124
802.5m	Fan Brycheiniog - Twr y Fan Foel	44
811m	Waun Fach	149
832m	Cadair Berwyn	15
854m	Arenig Fawr	7
872.2m	Moel Siabod	85
886m	Pen y Fan	125
892.7m	Cadair Idris - Penygadair	16
898m	Y Lliwedd	156
905m	Aran Fawddwy	5
917.5m	Tryfan	147
924m	Elidir Fawr	41
947m	Y Garn	153
1000.9m	Glyder Fawr	63
1064m	Carnedd Llewelyn	20
1085m	Snowdon - Yr Wyddfa	137

Equipment Checklist / Notes

Aberedw Hill

Height (m): 450.9m
OS Grid Reference: SO0844550775

Date	Parking ★ ★ ★ ★ ★	Map Ref: /1\
Ascent Start Time		Trig Time
Descent Start Time		Finish Time
Ascent Duration	Descent Duration	Total Time
Total Distance Covered		No. Of Steps
Companions		
Weather		

Enjoyment ○ ○ ○ ○ ○ ○ ○ ○ ○ ○
Views   ○ ○ ○ ○ ○ ○ ○ ○ ○ ○
Difficulty ○ ○ ○ ○ ○ ○ ○ ○ ○ ○

Highlights

Notes

Allt y Main

Height (m): 356m
OS Grid Reference: SJ1621115145

Date	Parking	☆☆☆☆☆	Map Ref: 2
Ascent Start Time		Trig Time	
Descent Start Time		Finish Time	
Ascent Duration	Descent Duration		Total Time
Total Distance Covered			No. Of Steps
Companions			
Weather			

Enjoyment ○○○○○○○○○○
Views ○○○○○○○○○○
Difficulty ○○○○○○○○○○

Highlights

Notes

Allt yr Esgair

Height (m): 392.6m
OS Grid Reference: SO1261324355

Date	Parking ☆☆☆☆☆	Map Ref: 3
Ascent Start Time	Trig Time	
Descent Start Time	Finish Time	
Ascent Duration	Descent Duration	Total Time
Total Distance Covered		No. Of Steps
Companions		

Weather

Enjoyment ○○○○○○○○○○
Views ○○○○○○○○○○
Difficulty ○○○○○○○○○○

Highlights

Notes

Allt-Fawr (Allt Fawr)

Height (m): 698m
OS Grid Reference: SH6817147460

Date	Parking ☆☆☆☆☆	Map Ref: 4
Ascent Start Time		Trig Time
Descent Start Time		Finish Time
Ascent Duration	Descent Duration	Total Time
Total Distance Covered		No. Of Steps
Companions		

Weather

Enjoyment ○○○○○○○○○○
Views ○○○○○○○○○○
Difficulty ○○○○○○○○○○

Highlights

Notes

Aran Fawddwy

Height (m): 905m
OS Grid Reference: SH8626922383

Date	Parking ☆☆☆☆☆	Map Ref: 5

Ascent Start Time | **Trig Time**

Descent Start Time | **Finish Time**

Ascent Duration | **Descent Duration** | **Total Time**

Total Distance Covered | **No. Of Steps**

Companions

Weather

Enjoyment ○○○○○○○○○○
Views ○○○○○○○○○○
Difficulty ○○○○○○○○○○

Highlights

Notes

Arenig Fach

Height (m): 689m
OS Grid Reference: SH8202741593

Date	Parking ★★★★★	Map Ref: 6
Ascent Start Time		Trig Time
Descent Start Time		Finish Time
Ascent Duration	Descent Duration	Total Time
Total Distance Covered		No. Of Steps
Companions		
Weather		

Enjoyment ○○○○○○○○○○
Views ○○○○○○○○○○
Difficulty ○○○○○○○○○○

Highlights

Notes

Arenig Fawr

Height (m): 854m
OS Grid Reference: SH8270436948

Date	Parking ☆☆☆☆☆	Map Ref: 7

Ascent Start Time	Trig Time

Descent Start Time	Finish Time

Ascent Duration	Descent Duration	Total Time

Total Distance Covered	No. Of Steps

Companions

Weather

Enjoyment ○○○○○○○○○○
Views ○○○○○○○○○○
Difficulty ○○○○○○○○○○

Highlights

Notes

Banc Llechwedd-mawr

Height (m): 560m
OS Grid Reference: SN7754189840

Date	Parking ☆☆☆☆☆	Map Ref: 8
Ascent Start Time		Trig Time
Descent Start Time		Finish Time
Ascent Duration	Descent Duration	Total Time
Total Distance Covered		No. Of Steps
Companions		

Weather

Enjoyment ○○○○○○○○○○
Views ○○○○○○○○○○
Difficulty ○○○○○○○○○○

Highlights

Notes

Beacon Hill

Height (m): 547m
OS Grid Reference: SO1764576794

Date	Parking ★ ★ ★ ★ ★	Map Ref: 9

Ascent Start Time | **Trig Time**

Descent Start Time | **Finish Time**

Ascent Duration | **Descent Duration** | **Total Time**

Total Distance Covered | **No. Of Steps**

Companions

Weather

Enjoyment ○ ○ ○ ○ ○ ○ ○ ○ ○ ○
Views ○ ○ ○ ○ ○ ○ ○ ○ ○ ○
Difficulty ○ ○ ○ ○ ○ ○ ○ ○ ○ ○

Highlights

Notes

Black Mountain

Height (m): 703.6m
OS Grid Reference: SO2552135385

Date	Parking ☆☆☆☆☆	Map Ref: 10
Ascent Start Time		Trig Time
Descent Start Time		Finish Time
Ascent Duration	Descent Duration	Total Time
Total Distance Covered		No. Of Steps
Companions		

Weather

Enjoyment ○○○○○○○○○○
Views ○○○○○○○○○○
Difficulty ○○○○○○○○○○

Highlights

Notes

Brandy Hill

Height (m): 206m
OS Grid Reference: SN2134313380

Date	Parking ★★★★★	Map Ref: 11
Ascent Start Time		Trig Time
Descent Start Time		Finish Time
Ascent Duration	Descent Duration	Total Time
Total Distance Covered		No. Of Steps
Companions		
Weather		

Enjoyment ○○○○○○○○○○
Views ○○○○○○○○○○
Difficulty ○○○○○○○○○○

Highlights

Notes

Bryn Amlwg

Height (m): 488m
OS Grid Reference: SN9215897342

Date	Parking ☆☆☆☆☆	Map Ref: /12/
Ascent Start Time		Trig Time
Descent Start Time		Finish Time
Ascent Duration	Descent Duration	Total Time
Total Distance Covered		No. Of Steps
Companions		
Weather		

Enjoyment ○ ○ ○ ○ ○ ○ ○ ○ ○ ○
Views ○ ○ ○ ○ ○ ○ ○ ○ ○ ○
Difficulty ○ ○ ○ ○ ○ ○ ○ ○ ○ ○

Highlights

Notes

Bryn Arw

Height (m): 385m
OS Grid Reference: SO3015520698

Date	Parking ☆☆☆☆☆	Map Ref: /13\

Ascent Start Time | **Trig Time**

Descent Start Time | **Finish Time**

Ascent Duration | **Descent Duration** | **Total Time**

Total Distance Covered | **No. Of Steps**

Companions

Weather

Enjoyment ○○○○○○○○○○
Views ○○○○○○○○○○
Difficulty ○○○○○○○○○○

Highlights

Notes

Bryn y Fan

Height (m): 482m
OS Grid Reference: SN9312388496

Date	Parking ☆☆☆☆☆	Map Ref: 14
Ascent Start Time		Trig Time
Descent Start Time		Finish Time
Ascent Duration	Descent Duration	Total Time
Total Distance Covered		No. Of Steps
Companions		

Weather

Enjoyment ○○○○○○○○○○
Views ○○○○○○○○○○
Difficulty ○○○○○○○○○○

Highlights

Notes

Cadair Berwyn

Height (m): 832m
OS Grid Reference: SJ0716332351

Date	Parking	☆☆☆☆☆	Map Ref: /15

Ascent Start Time		Trig Time	
Descent Start Time		Finish Time	
Ascent Duration	Descent Duration		Total Time
Total Distance Covered		No. Of Steps	
Companions			

Weather

Enjoyment ○○○○○○○○○○
Views ○○○○○○○○○○
Difficulty ○○○○○○○○○○

Highlights

Notes

Cadair Idris - Penygadair

Height (m): 892.7m
OS Grid Reference: SH7111413035

Date	Parking ☆☆☆☆☆	Map Ref: /16\
Ascent Start Time	Trig Time	
Descent Start Time	Finish Time	
Ascent Duration	Descent Duration	Total Time
Total Distance Covered		No. Of Steps
Companions		

Weather

Enjoyment ○○○○○○○○○○
Views ○○○○○○○○○○
Difficulty ○○○○○○○○○○

Highlights

Notes

Caeliber Isaf

Height (m): 353.5m
OS Grid Reference: SO2116393413

Date	Parking ☆☆☆☆☆	Map Ref: 17
Ascent Start Time		Trig Time
Descent Start Time		Finish Time
Ascent Duration	Descent Duration	Total Time
Total Distance Covered		No. Of Steps
Companions		
Weather		

Enjoutment ○○○○○○○○○○
Views ○○○○○○○○○○
Difficulty ○○○○○○○○○○

Highlights

Notes

Carn Fadryn

Height (m): 371m
OS Grid Reference: SH2786535182

Date	Parking ☆☆☆☆☆	Map Ref: 18
Ascent Start Time		Trig Time
Descent Start Time		Finish Time
Ascent Duration	Descent Duration	Total Time
Total Distance Covered		No. Of Steps
Companions		
Weather		

Enjoyment ○ ○ ○ ○ ○ ○ ○ ○ ○ ○
Views ○ ○ ○ ○ ○ ○ ○ ○ ○ ○
Difficulty ○ ○ ○ ○ ○ ○ ○ ○ ○ ○

Highlights

Notes

Carn Gafallt

Height (m): 466m
OS Grid Reference: SN9400564643

Date	Parking ★★★★★	Map Ref: /19\

Ascent Start Time | **Trig Time**

Descent Start Time | **Finish Time**

Ascent Duration | **Descent Duration** | **Total Time**

Total Distance Covered | **No. Of Steps**

Companions

Weather

Enjoyment ○○○○○○○○○○
Views ○○○○○○○○○○
Difficulty ○○○○○○○○○○

Highlights

Notes

Carnedd Llewelyn

Height (m): 1064m
OS Grid Reference: SH6836164372

Date	Parking	Map Ref: 20
Ascent Start Time		Trig Time
Descent Start Time		Finish Time
Ascent Duration	Descent Duration	Total Time
Total Distance Covered		No. Of Steps
Companions		

Weather

Enjoyment ○○○○○○○○○○
Views ○○○○○○○○○○
Difficulty ○○○○○○○○○○

Highlights

Notes

Carnedd Wen

Height (m): 523m
OS Grid Reference: SH9240509917

Date	Parking ★★★★★	Map Ref: 21

Ascent Start Time | **Trig Time**

Descent Start Time | **Finish Time**

Ascent Duration | **Descent Duration** | **Total Time**

Total Distance Covered | **No. Of Steps**

Companions

Weather

Enjoyment ○○○○○○○○○○
Views ○○○○○○○○○○
Difficulty ○○○○○○○○○○

Highlights

Notes

Carnedd y Filiast

Height (m): 669m
OS Grid Reference: SH8711644596

Date	Parking ★★★★★	Map Ref: 22
Ascent Start Time		Trig Time
Descent Start Time		Finish Time
Ascent Duration	Descent Duration	Total Time
Total Distance Covered		No. Of Steps
Companions		

Weather

Enjoyment ○○○○○○○○○○
Views ○○○○○○○○○○
Difficulty ○○○○○○○○○○

Highlights

Notes

Carneddau

Height (m): 445m
OS Grid Reference: SO0699155197

| Date | Parking | ☆☆☆☆☆ | Map Ref: 23 |

Ascent Start Time | Trig Time
Descent Start Time | Finish Time
Ascent Duration | Descent Duration | Total Time
Total Distance Covered | No. Of Steps
Companions

Weather

Enjoyment ○○○○○○○○○○
Views ○○○○○○○○○○
Difficulty ○○○○○○○○○○

Highlights

Notes

Carneddol

Height (m): 235.9m
OS Grid Reference: SH3011533096

Date	Parking ☆☆☆☆☆	Map Ref: 24

Ascent Start Time | **Trig Time**

Descent Start Time | **Finish Time**

Ascent Duration | **Descent Duration** | **Total Time**

Total Distance Covered | **No. Of Steps**

Companions

Weather

Enjoyment ○○○○○○○○○○
Views ○○○○○○○○○○
Difficulty ○○○○○○○○○○

Highlights

Notes

Cefn Cenarth

Height (m): 460m
OS Grid Reference: SN9690576263

Date	Parking ★★★★★	Map Ref: 25

Ascent Start Time	Trig Time

Descent Start Time	Finish Time

Ascent Duration	Descent Duration	Total Time

Total Distance Covered	No. Of Steps

Companions

Weather

Enjoyment ○○○○○○○○○
Views ○○○○○○○○○
Difficulty ○○○○○○○○○

Highlights

Notes

Cefn Eglwysilan

Height (m): 382m
OS Grid Reference: ST0970990506

Date	Parking ☆☆☆☆☆	Map Ref: 26
Ascent Start Time		Trig Time
Descent Start Time		Finish Time
Ascent Duration	Descent Duration	Total Time
Total Distance Covered		No. Of Steps
Companions		

Weather

Enjoyment ○○○○○○○○○○
Views ○○○○○○○○○○
Difficulty ○○○○○○○○○○

Highlights

Notes

Cefn yr Ystrad

Height (m): 617.3m
OS Grid Reference: SO0869513732

Date	Parking ★★★★★	Map Ref: /27/
Ascent Start Time		Trig Time
Descent Start Time		Finish Time
Ascent Duration	Descent Duration	Total Time
Total Distance Covered		No. Of Steps
Companions		

Weather

Enjoyment ○○○○○○○○○○
Views ○○○○○○○○○○
Difficulty ○○○○○○○○○○

Highlights

Notes

Coety Mountain (Mynydd Coety)

Height (m): 578m
OS Grid Reference: SO2315907991

Date	Parking ☆☆☆☆☆	Map Ref: 28

Ascent Start Time | **Trig Time**

Descent Start Time | **Finish Time**

Ascent Duration | **Descent Duration** | **Total Time**

Total Distance Covered | **No. Of Steps**

Companions

Weather

Enjoyment ○○○○○○○○○○
Views ○○○○○○○○○○
Difficulty ○○○○○○○○○○

Highlights

Notes

Corndon Hill

Height (m): 513.6m
OS Grid Reference: SO3060096923

Date	Parking ★★★★★	Map Ref: 29
Ascent Start Time	Trig Time	
Descent Start Time	Finish Time	
Ascent Duration	Descent Duration	Total Time
Total Distance Covered		No. Of Steps
Companions		
Weather		

Enjoreyment ○ ○ ○ ○ ○ ○ ○ ○ ○ ○
Views ○ ○ ○ ○ ○ ○ ○ ○ ○ ○
Difficulty ○ ○ ○ ○ ○ ○ ○ ○ ○ ○

Highlights

Notes

Craig Cwm Silyn

Height (m): 734m
OS Grid Reference: SH5255650264

Date	Parking	Map Ref: 30
Ascent Start Time		Trig Time
Descent Start Time		Finish Time
Ascent Duration	Descent Duration	Total Time
Total Distance Covered		No. Of Steps
Companions		
Weather		

Enjoncyment ○○○○○○○○○○
Views ○○○○○○○○○○
Difficulty ○○○○○○○○○○

Highlights

Notes

Craig Goch (Mynydd Cwmcelli)

Height (m): 468.3m
OS Grid Reference: SH8045809954

Date	Parking ☆☆☆☆☆	Map Ref: 31

Ascent Start Time	Trig Time

Descent Start Time	Finish Time

Ascent Duration	Descent Duration	Total Time

Total Distance Covered	No. Of Steps

Companions

Weather

Enjoyment ○○○○○○○○○○
Views ○○○○○○○○○○
Difficulty ○○○○○○○○○○

Highlights

Notes

Craig y Castell

Height (m): 321m
OS Grid Reference: SH6977916199

Date	Parking ☆☆☆☆☆	Map Ref: /32\
Ascent Start Time		Trig Time
Descent Start Time		Finish Time
Ascent Duration	Descent Duration	Total Time
Total Distance Covered		No. Of Steps

Companions

Weather

Enjoompany ○○○○○○○○○○
Views ○○○○○○○○○○
Difficulty ○○○○○○○○○○

Highlights

Notes

Craig y Llyn

Height (m): 600m
OS Grid Reference: SN9068503153

Date	Parking ★★★★★	Map Ref: 33
Ascent Start Time		Trig Time
Descent Start Time		Finish Time
Ascent Duration	Descent Duration	Total Time
Total Distance Covered		No. Of Steps
Companions		

Weather

Enjoyment ○○○○○○○○○○
Views ○○○○○○○○○○
Difficulty ○○○○○○○○○○

Highlights

Notes

Craig yr Allt

Height (m): 273m
OS Grid Reference: ST1333185061

Date	Parking ★ ★ ★ ★ ★	Map Ref: /34\
Ascent Start Time		Trig Time
Descent Start Time		Finish Time
Ascent Duration	Descent Duration	Total Time
Total Distance Covered		No. Of Steps
Companions		

Weather

Enjoyment ○ ○ ○ ○ ○ ○ ○ ○ ○ ○
Views   ○ ○ ○ ○ ○ ○ ○ ○ ○ ○
Difficulty ○ ○ ○ ○ ○ ○ ○ ○ ○ ○

Highlights

Notes

Creigiau Gleision

Height (m): 678m
OS Grid Reference: SH7289961537

Date	Parking ★★★★★	Map Ref: /35\

Ascent Start Time	Trig Time

Descent Start Time	Finish Time

Ascent Duration	Descent Duration	Total Time

Total Distance Covered	No. Of Steps

Companions

Weather

- Enjoyment ○○○○○○○○○○
- Views ○○○○○○○○○○
- Difficulty ○○○○○○○○○○

Highlights

Notes

Crugiau Merched

Height (m): 462m
OS Grid Reference: SN7221845536

Date	Parking ★★★★★	Map Ref: /36\
Ascent Start Time		Trig Time
Descent Start Time		Finish Time
Ascent Duration	Descent Duration	Total Time
Total Distance Covered		No. Of Steps
Companions		
Weather		

Enjoyment ○○○○○○○○○○
Views ○○○○○○○○○○
Difficulty ○○○○○○○○○○

Highlights

Notes

Cyrn-y-Brain

Height (m): 564.6m
OS Grid Reference: SJ2081948882

Date	Parking ☆☆☆☆☆	Map Ref: 37
Ascent Start Time	Trig Time	
Descent Start Time	Finish Time	
Ascent Duration	Descent Duration	Total Time
Total Distance Covered	No. Of Steps	
Companions		

Weather

Enjoyment ○○○○○○○○○○
Views ○○○○○○○○○○
Difficulty ○○○○○○○○○○

Highlights

Notes

Disgwylfa Fawr

Height (m): 507m
OS Grid Reference: SN7372984739

Date	Parking ☆☆☆☆☆	Map Ref: 38
Ascent Start Time		Trig Time
Descent Start Time		Finish Time
Ascent Duration	Descent Duration	Total Time
Total Distance Covered		No. Of Steps
Companions		
Weather		

Enjoyment ○ ○ ○ ○ ○ ○ ○ ○ ○ ○
Views   ○ ○ ○ ○ ○ ○ ○ ○ ○ ○
Difficulty ○ ○ ○ ○ ○ ○ ○ ○ ○ ○

Highlights

Notes

Drosgol

Height (m): 550m
OS Grid Reference: SN7595987858

Date	Parking ★★★★★	Map Ref: 39

Ascent Start Time	Trig Time

Descent Start Time	Finish Time

Ascent Duration	Descent Duration	Total Time

Total Distance Covered	No. Of Steps

Companions

Weather

Enjoyment ○○○○○○○○○○
Views ○○○○○○○○○○
Difficulty ○○○○○○○○○○

Highlights

Notes

Drygarn Fawr

Height (m): 645m
OS Grid Reference: SN8628758409

Date	Parking ★ ★ ★ ★ ★	Map Ref: /40\
Ascent Start Time		Trig Time
Descent Start Time		Finish Time
Ascent Duration	Descent Duration	Total Time
Total Distance Covered		No. Of Steps
Companions		
Weather		

Enjoyment ○ ○ ○ ○ ○ ○ ○ ○ ○ ○
Views ○ ○ ○ ○ ○ ○ ○ ○ ○ ○
Difficulty ○ ○ ○ ○ ○ ○ ○ ○ ○ ○

Highlights

Notes

Elidir Fawr

Height (m): 924m
OS Grid Reference: SH6117361289

Date	Parking ☆☆☆☆☆	Map Ref: 41

Ascent Start Time | **Trig Time**

Descent Start Time | **Finish Time**

Ascent Duration | **Descent Duration** | **Total Time**

Total Distance Covered | **No. Of Steps**

Companions

Weather

- Enjoyment ○○○○○○○○○○
- Views ○○○○○○○○○○
- Difficulty ○○○○○○○○○○

Highlights

Notes

Esgair Ddu

Height (m): 464m
OS Grid Reference: SH8732510641

Date	Parking ★★★★★	Map Ref: 42

Ascent Start Time	Trig Time

Descent Start Time	Finish Time

Ascent Duration	Descent Duration	Total Time

Total Distance Covered	No. Of Steps

Companions

Weather

Enjoyment ○○○○○○○○○○
Views   ○○○○○○○○○○
Difficulty ○○○○○○○○○○

Highlights

Notes

Esgeiriau Gwynion (Foel Rhudd)

Height (m): 671m
OS Grid Reference: SH8894723639

| Date | Parking ★★★★★ | Map Ref: 43 |

Ascent Start Time | Trig Time

Descent Start Time | Finish Time

Ascent Duration | Descent Duration | Total Time

Total Distance Covered | No. Of Steps

Companions

Weather

Enjoyment ○○○○○○○○○○
Views ○○○○○○○○○○
Difficulty ○○○○○○○○○○

Highlights

Notes

Fan Brycheiniog - Twr y Fan Foel

Height (m): 802.5m
OS Grid Reference: SN8243422060

Date	Parking ☆☆☆☆☆	Map Ref: /44\
Ascent Start Time		Trig Time
Descent Start Time		Finish Time
Ascent Duration	Descent Duration	Total Time
Total Distance Covered		No. Of Steps
Companions		
Weather		

Enjoracic ○○○○○○○○○○
Views ○○○○○○○○○○
Difficulty ○○○○○○○○○○

Highlights

Notes

Fan Fawr

Height (m): 734m
OS Grid Reference: SN9698719364

| Date | Parking ☆☆☆☆☆ | Map Ref: 45 |

Ascent Start Time | **Trig Time**

Descent Start Time | **Finish Time**

Ascent Duration | **Descent Duration** | **Total Time**

Total Distance Covered | **No. Of Steps**

Companions

Weather

Enjoyment ○○○○○○○○○○
Views ○○○○○○○○○○
Difficulty ○○○○○○○○○○

Highlights

Notes

Fan Gyhirych

Height (m): 725m
OS Grid Reference: SN8805419119

Date	Parking ☆☆☆☆☆	Map Ref: 46
Ascent Start Time		Trig Time
Descent Start Time		Finish Time
Ascent Duration	Descent Duration	Total Time
Total Distance Covered		No. Of Steps
Companions		

Weather

Enjoment ○○○○○○○○○○
Views ○○○○○○○○○○
Difficulty ○○○○○○○○○○

Highlights

Notes

Fan Nedd

Height (m): 663m
OS Grid Reference: SN9133218408

Date	Parking	Map Ref: 47
Ascent Start Time		Trig Time
Descent Start Time		Finish Time
Ascent Duration	Descent Duration	Total Time
Total Distance Covered		No. Of Steps
Companions		
Weather		

- Enjoyment
- Views
- Difficulty

Highlights

Notes

Ffridd Cocyn

Height (m): 312.8m
OS Grid Reference: SH6245604290

Date	Parking ★★★★★	Map Ref: 48
Ascent Start Time		Trig Time
Descent Start Time		Finish Time
Ascent Duration	Descent Duration	Total Time
Total Distance Covered		No. Of Steps
Companions		

Weather

Enjoyment ○○○○○○○○○○
Views ○○○○○○○○○○
Difficulty ○○○○○○○○○○

Highlights

Notes

Foel Cae'rberllan

Height (m): 380m
OS Grid Reference: SH6762708209

Date	Parking ☆☆☆☆☆	Map Ref: /49
Ascent Start Time		Trig Time
Descent Start Time		Finish Time
Ascent Duration	Descent Duration	Total Time
Total Distance Covered		No. Of Steps
Companions		

Weather

Enjoyment ○○○○○○○○○○
Views ○○○○○○○○○○
Difficulty ○○○○○○○○○○

Highlights

Notes

Foel Cedig

Height (m): 667.4m
OS Grid Reference: SH9817028327

Date	Parking ☆☆☆☆☆	Map Ref: /50\
Ascent Start Time		Trig Time
Descent Start Time		Finish Time
Ascent Duration	Descent Duration	Total Time
Total Distance Covered		No. Of Steps

Companions

Weather

Enjoyment ○○○○○○○○○○
Views ○○○○○○○○○○
Difficulty ○○○○○○○○○○

Highlights

Notes

Foel Cwmcerwyn

Height (m): 536m
OS Grid Reference: SN0940731156

Date	Parking ☆☆☆☆☆	Map Ref: 51
Ascent Start Time		Trig Time
Descent Start Time		Finish Time
Ascent Duration	Descent Duration	Total Time
Total Distance Covered		No. Of Steps
Companions		
Weather		

Enjoyment ○○○○○○○○○○
Views ○○○○○○○○○○
Difficulty ○○○○○○○○○○

Highlights

Notes

Foel Fenlli

Height (m): 510.9m
OS Grid Reference: SJ1648360078

Date	Parking ★★★★★	Map Ref: /52
Ascent Start Time		Trig Time
Descent Start Time		Finish Time
Ascent Duration	Descent Duration	Total Time
Total Distance Covered		No. Of Steps
Companions		

Weather

Enjoyment ○ ○ ○ ○ ○ ○ ○ ○ ○ ○
Views   ○ ○ ○ ○ ○ ○ ○ ○ ○ ○
Difficulty ○ ○ ○ ○ ○ ○ ○ ○ ○ ○

Highlights

Notes

Foel Fynyddau

Height (m): 370m
OS Grid Reference: SS7828493601

Date	Parking ☆☆☆☆☆	Map Ref: /53\
Ascent Start Time		Trig Time
Descent Start Time		Finish Time
Ascent Duration	Descent Duration	Total Time
Total Distance Covered		No. Of Steps
Companions		
Weather		

Enjoyment ○○○○○○○○○○
Views ○○○○○○○○○○
Difficulty ○○○○○○○○○○

Highlights

Notes

Foel Goch

Height (m): 611m
OS Grid Reference: SH9537942292

Date	Parking ☆☆☆☆☆	Map Ref: 54
Ascent Start Time		Trig Time
Descent Start Time		Finish Time
Ascent Duration	Descent Duration	Total Time
Total Distance Covered		No. Of Steps

Companions

Weather

Enjoyment ○○○○○○○○○○
Views ○○○○○○○○○○
Difficulty ○○○○○○○○○○

Highlights

Notes

Foel Offrwm

Height (m): 405m
OS Grid Reference: SH7498420987

Date	Parking ☆☆☆☆☆	Map Ref: /55\
Ascent Start Time		Trig Time
Descent Start Time		Finish Time
Ascent Duration	Descent Duration	Total Time
Total Distance Covered		No. Of Steps
Companions		

Weather

- Enjoyment ○○○○○○○○○
- Views ○○○○○○○○○
- Difficulty ○○○○○○○○○

Highlights

Notes

Frenni Fawr

Height (m): 395m
OS Grid Reference: SN2029734911

Date	Parking ★★★★★	Map Ref: 56
Ascent Start Time		Trig Time
Descent Start Time		Finish Time
Ascent Duration	Descent Duration	Total Time
Total Distance Covered		No. Of Steps
Companions		

Weather

Enjoyment ○○○○○○○○○○
Views ○○○○○○○○○○
Difficulty ○○○○○○○○○○

Highlights

Notes

Gamallt

Height (m): 288m
OS Grid Reference: SH6655006761

Date	Parking ☆☆☆☆☆	Map Ref: 57
Ascent Start Time		Trig Time
Descent Start Time		Finish Time
Ascent Duration	Descent Duration	Total Time
Total Distance Covered		No. Of Steps
Companions		
Weather		

Enjoyment ○○○○○○○○○○
Views ○○○○○○○○○○
Difficulty ○○○○○○○○○○

Highlights

Notes

Garn Boduan

Height (m): 279m
OS Grid Reference: SH3120739347

Date	Parking ★★★★★	Map Ref: 58

Ascent Start Time		Trig Time	
Descent Start Time		Finish Time	
Ascent Duration	Descent Duration		Total Time
Total Distance Covered		No. Of Steps	
Companions			

Weather

Enjoyment ○○○○○○○○○○
Views ○○○○○○○○○○
Difficulty ○○○○○○○○○○

Highlights

Notes

Garreg Lwyd

Height (m): 498.1m
OS Grid Reference: SN9421473327

Date	Parking ☆☆☆☆☆	Map Ref: 59

Ascent Start Time | **Trig Time**

Descent Start Time | **Finish Time**

Ascent Duration | **Descent Duration** | **Total Time**

Total Distance Covered | **No. Of Steps**

Companions

Weather

Enjoyment ○○○○○○○○○○
Views ○○○○○○○○○○
Difficulty ○○○○○○○○○○

Highlights

Notes

Garreg-hir

Height (m): 484.9m
OS Grid Reference: SN9986997916

Date	Parking ★★★★★	Map Ref: /60\
Ascent Start Time		Trig Time
Descent Start Time		Finish Time
Ascent Duration	Descent Duration	Total Time
Total Distance Covered		No. Of Steps
Companions		

Weather

- Enjoyment ○○○○○○○○○○
- Views ○○○○○○○○○○
- Difficulty ○○○○○○○○○○

Highlights

Notes

Garth Hill

Height (m): 307m
OS Grid Reference: ST1033983500

| Date | Parking ☆☆☆☆☆ | Map Ref: 61 |

Ascent Start Time | **Trig Time**

Descent Start Time | **Finish Time**

Ascent Duration | **Descent Duration** | **Total Time**

Total Distance Covered | **No. Of Steps**

Companions

Weather

Enjoyment ○○○○○○○○○○
Views ○○○○○○○○○○
Difficulty ○○○○○○○○○○

Highlights

Notes

Glasgwm

Height (m): 779m
OS Grid Reference: SH8367419455

Date	Parking ☆☆☆☆☆	Map Ref: /62\

Ascent Start Time | **Trig Time**

Descent Start Time | **Finish Time**

Ascent Duration | **Descent Duration** | **Total Time**

Total Distance Covered | **No. Of Steps**

Companions

Weather

Enjoyment ○○○○○○○○○○
Views ○○○○○○○○○○
Difficulty ○○○○○○○○○○

Highlights

Notes

Glyder Fawr

Height (m): 1000.9m
OS Grid Reference: SH6424357953

Date	Parking ☆☆☆☆☆	Map Ref: /63/
Ascent Start Time		Trig Time
Descent Start Time		Finish Time
Ascent Duration	Descent Duration	Total Time
Total Distance Covered		No. Of Steps
Companions		
Weather		

Enjoyment ○○○○○○○○○○
Views ○○○○○○○○○○
Difficulty ○○○○○○○○○○

Highlights

Notes

Graig Syfyrddin (Edmund's Tump)

Height (m): 423m
OS Grid Reference: SO4039121066

Date	Parking ★★★★★	Map Ref: /64\
Ascent Start Time		Trig Time
Descent Start Time		Finish Time
Ascent Duration	Descent Duration	Total Time
Total Distance Covered		No. Of Steps
Companions		
Weather		

Enjoyment ○○○○○○○○○○
Views ○○○○○○○○○○
Difficulty ○○○○○○○○○○

Highlights

Notes

Great Orme

Height (m): 207.1m
OS Grid Reference: SH7675183334

Date	Parking ☆☆☆☆☆	Map Ref: /65
Ascent Start Time		Trig Time
Descent Start Time		Finish Time
Ascent Duration	Descent Duration	Total Time
Total Distance Covered		No. Of Steps
Companions		
Weather		

Enjoyment ○○○○○○○○○○
Views ○○○○○○○○○○
Difficulty ○○○○○○○○○○

Highlights

Notes

Great Rhos

Height (m): 660m
OS Grid Reference: SO1821863897

Date	Parking	☆☆☆☆☆	Map Ref: /66
Ascent Start Time		Trig Time	
Descent Start Time		Finish Time	
Ascent Duration	Descent Duration	Total Time	
Total Distance Covered		No. Of Steps	
Companions			

Weather

Enjoyment ○○○○○○○○○○
Views ○○○○○○○○○○
Difficulty ○○○○○○○○○○

Highlights

Notes

Gwastedyn Hill

Height (m): 477m
OS Grid Reference: SN9868166145

Date	Parking ★★★★★	Map Ref: 67
Ascent Start Time		Trig Time
Descent Start Time		Finish Time
Ascent Duration	Descent Duration	Total Time
Total Distance Covered		No. Of Steps
Companions		
Weather		

Enjoyment ○○○○○○○○○○
Views ○○○○○○○○○○
Difficulty ○○○○○○○○○○

Highlights

Notes

Gwauncestre Hill

Height (m): 542m
OS Grid Reference: SO1582055548

Date	Parking ☆☆☆☆☆	Map Ref: 68

Ascent Start Time | **Trig Time**

Descent Start Time | **Finish Time**

Ascent Duration | **Descent Duration** | **Total Time**

Total Distance Covered | **No. Of Steps**

Companions

Weather

Enjoyment ○○○○○○○○○○
Views ○○○○○○○○○○
Difficulty ○○○○○○○○○○

Highlights

Notes

Gyrn Ddu

Height (m): 522.1m
OS Grid Reference: SH4011546785

Date	Parking ☆☆☆☆☆	Map Ref: 69
Ascent Start Time		Trig Time
Descent Start Time		Finish Time
Ascent Duration	Descent Duration	Total Time
Total Distance Covered		No. Of Steps
Companions		
Weather		

- Enjoyment ○○○○○○○○○○
- Views ○○○○○○○○○○
- Difficulty ○○○○○○○○○○

Highlights

Notes

Gyrn Moelfre

Height (m): 523m
OS Grid Reference: SJ1844429384

| Date | Parking ★★★★★ | Map Ref: 70 |

Ascent Start Time | Trig Time

Descent Start Time | Finish Time

Ascent Duration | Descent Duration | Total Time

Total Distance Covered | No. Of Steps

Companions

Weather

Enjoyment ○○○○○○○○○○
Views ○○○○○○○○○○
Difficulty ○○○○○○○○○○

Highlights

Notes

Hafod Ithel

Height (m): 361m
OS Grid Reference: SN6106267794

Date	Parking ☆☆☆☆☆	Map Ref: /71

Ascent Start Time | **Trig Time**

Descent Start Time | **Finish Time**

Ascent Duration | **Descent Duration** | **Total Time**

Total Distance Covered | **No. Of Steps**

Companions

Weather

Enjoyment ○○○○○○○○○○
Views ○○○○○○○○○○
Difficulty ○○○○○○○○○○

Highlights

Notes

Hirfynydd

Height (m): 481m
OS Grid Reference: SN8394507610

Date	Parking ☆☆☆☆☆	Map Ref: 72
Ascent Start Time		Trig Time
Descent Start Time		Finish Time
Ascent Duration	Descent Duration	Total Time
Total Distance Covered		No. Of Steps

Companions

Weather

Enjoyment ○○○○○○○○○○
Views ○○○○○○○○○○
Difficulty ○○○○○○○○○○

Highlights

Notes

Holyhead Mountain

Height (m): 220m
OS Grid Reference: SH2185582945

Date	Parking ★★★★★	Map Ref: /73/
Ascent Start Time		Trig Time
Descent Start Time		Finish Time
Ascent Duration	Descent Duration	Total Time
Total Distance Covered		No. Of Steps
Companions		

Weather

- Enjoyment ○○○○○○○○○○
- Views ○○○○○○○○○○
- Difficulty ○○○○○○○○○○

Highlights

Notes

Hope Mountain

Height (m): 330m
OS Grid Reference: SJ2947956896

Date	Parking ★★★★★	Map Ref: 74
Ascent Start Time		Trig Time
Descent Start Time		Finish Time
Ascent Duration	Descent Duration	Total Time
Total Distance Covered		No. Of Steps
Companions		

Weather

Enjoyment ○○○○○○○○○○
Views ○○○○○○○○○○
Difficulty ○○○○○○○○○○

Highlights

Notes

Llan Ddu Fawr (Waun Claerddu) ✓

Height (m): 594m
OS Grid Reference: SN7906870423

Date	Parking ★★★★★	Map Ref: /75\
Ascent Start Time	Trig Time	
Descent Start Time	Finish Time	
Ascent Duration	Descent Duration	Total Time
Total Distance Covered	No. Of Steps	
Companions		

Weather

- Enjoyment ○○○○○○○○○○
- Views ○○○○○○○○○○
- Difficulty ○○○○○○○○○○

Highlights

Notes

Long Mountain

Height (m): 408m
OS Grid Reference: SJ2647405823

Date	Parking ★★★★★	Map Ref: /76\
Ascent Start Time		Trig Time
Descent Start Time		Finish Time
Ascent Duration	Descent Duration	Total Time
Total Distance Covered		No. Of Steps
Companions		

Weather

Enjoyment ○○○○○○○○○○
Views ○○○○○○○○○○
Difficulty ○○○○○○○○○○

Highlights

Notes

Maesglase

Height (m): 678.5m
OS Grid Reference: SH8172915033

Date	Parking ☆☆☆☆☆	Map Ref: /77/
Ascent Start Time	Trig Time	
Descent Start Time	Finish Time	
Ascent Duration	Descent Duration	Total Time
Total Distance Covered		No. Of Steps
Companions		
Weather		

Enjoyment ○ ○ ○ ○ ○ ○ ○ ○ ○ ○
Views   ○ ○ ○ ○ ○ ○ ○ ○ ○ ○
Difficulty ○ ○ ○ ○ ○ ○ ○ ○ ○ ○

Highlights

Notes

Manod Mawr

Height (m): 661m
OS Grid Reference: SH7243944664

Date	Parking ★ ★ ★ ★ ★	Map Ref: /78\
Ascent Start Time		Trig Time
Descent Start Time		Finish Time
Ascent Duration	Descent Duration	Total Time
Total Distance Covered		No. Of Steps
Companions		

Weather

Enjoracle ○ ○ ○ ○ ○ ○ ○ ○ ○ ○
Views ○ ○ ○ ○ ○ ○ ○ ○ ○ ○
Difficulty ○ ○ ○ ○ ○ ○ ○ ○ ○ ○

Highlights

Notes

Moel Cynghorion

Height (m): 674m
OS Grid Reference: SH5860756392

| Date | Parking ☆☆☆☆☆ | Map Ref: 79 |

Ascent Start Time | **Trig Time**

Descent Start Time | **Finish Time**

Ascent Duration | **Descent Duration** | **Total Time**

Total Distance Covered | **No. Of Steps**

Companions

Weather

Enjoment ○ ○ ○ ○ ○ ○ ○ ○ ○ ○
Views   ○ ○ ○ ○ ○ ○ ○ ○ ○ ○
Difficulty ○ ○ ○ ○ ○ ○ ○ ○ ○ ○

Highlights

Notes

Moel Eilio

Height (m): 726m
OS Grid Reference: SH5557857715

Date	Parking ★★★★★	Map Ref: 80

Ascent Start Time	Trig Time

Descent Start Time	Finish Time

Ascent Duration	Descent Duration	Total Time

Total Distance Covered	No. Of Steps

Companions

Weather

Enjoyment ○○○○○○○○○○
Views ○○○○○○○○○○
Difficulty ○○○○○○○○○○

Highlights

Notes

Moel Famau

Height (m): 554.8m
OS Grid Reference: SJ1612262671

Date	Parking ★ ★ ★ ★ ★	Map Ref: /81/
Ascent Start Time		Trig Time
Descent Start Time		Finish Time
Ascent Duration	Descent Duration	Total Time
Total Distance Covered		No. Of Steps
Companions		
Weather		

Enjoyment   ○ ○ ○ ○ ○ ○ ○ ○ ○ ○
Views   ○ ○ ○ ○ ○ ○ ○ ○ ○ ○
Difficulty ○ ○ ○ ○ ○ ○ ○ ○ ○ ○

Highlights

Notes

Moel Gyw

Height (m): 467m
OS Grid Reference: SJ1715157544

Date	Parking ★★★★★	Map Ref: /82\
Ascent Start Time		Trig Time
Descent Start Time		Finish Time
Ascent Duration	Descent Duration	Total Time
Total Distance Covered		No. Of Steps
Companions		
Weather		

Enjorment ○○○○○○○○○○
Views ○○○○○○○○○○
Difficulty ○○○○○○○○○○

Highlights

Notes

Moel Hebog

Height (m): 783m
OS Grid Reference: SH5648246940

Date	Parking ★★★★★	Map Ref: 83

Ascent Start Time	Trig Time

Descent Start Time	Finish Time

Ascent Duration	Descent Duration	Total Time

Total Distance Covered	No. Of Steps

Companions

Weather

Enjoyment ○○○○○○○○○○
Views ○○○○○○○○○○
Difficulty ○○○○○○○○○○

Highlights

Notes

Moel Llyfnant

Height (m): 751m
OS Grid Reference: SH8082835185

| Date | Parking ★ ★ ★ ★ ★ | Map Ref: 84 |

Ascent Start Time | Trig Time

Descent Start Time | Finish Time

Ascent Duration | Descent Duration | Total Time

Total Distance Covered | No. Of Steps

Companions

Weather

Enjoyment ○ ○ ○ ○ ○ ○ ○ ○ ○ ○
Views ○ ○ ○ ○ ○ ○ ○ ○ ○ ○
Difficulty ○ ○ ○ ○ ○ ○ ○ ○ ○ ○

Highlights

Notes

Moel Siabod

Height (m): 872.2m
OS Grid Reference: SH7052454631

Date	Parking ☆☆☆☆☆	Map Ref: 85
Ascent Start Time		Trig Time
Descent Start Time		Finish Time
Ascent Duration	Descent Duration	Total Time
Total Distance Covered		No. Of Steps
Companions		
Weather		

Enjoring ○○○○○○○○○
Views ○○○○○○○○○
Difficulty ○○○○○○○○○

Highlights

Notes

Moel y Dyniewyd

Height (m): 382.4m
OS Grid Reference: SH6126647735

Date	Parking ★★★★★	Map Ref: /86\

Ascent Start Time	Trig Time

Descent Start Time	Finish Time

Ascent Duration	Descent Duration	Total Time

Total Distance Covered	No. Of Steps

Companions

Weather

Enjoyment ○○○○○○○○○○
Views ○○○○○○○○○○
Difficulty ○○○○○○○○○○

Highlights

Notes

Moel y Gamelin

Height (m): 576.9m
OS Grid Reference: SJ1763446517

Date	Parking ★★★★★	Map Ref: 87

Ascent Start Time | **Trig Time**

Descent Start Time | **Finish Time**

Ascent Duration | **Descent Duration** | **Total Time**

Total Distance Covered | **No. Of Steps**

Companions

Weather

- Enjoyment ○○○○○○○○○○
- Views ○○○○○○○○○○
- Difficulty ○○○○○○○○○○

Highlights

Notes

Moel y Golfa

Height (m): 403.2m
OS Grid Reference: SJ2907412529

Date	Parking ★★★★★	Map Ref: /88
Ascent Start Time		Trig Time
Descent Start Time		Finish Time
Ascent Duration	Descent Duration	Total Time
Total Distance Covered		No. Of Steps
Companions		

Weather

Enjoyment ○○○○○○○○○○
Views ○○○○○○○○○○
Difficulty ○○○○○○○○○○

Highlights

Notes

Moel Ysgyfarnogod

Height (m): 623m
OS Grid Reference: SH6584234590

Date	Parking ☆☆☆☆☆	Map Ref: /89

Ascent Start Time — Trig Time

Descent Start Time — Finish Time

Ascent Duration | **Descent Duration** | **Total Time**

Total Distance Covered — No. Of Steps

Companions

Weather

Enjoyment ○○○○○○○○○
Views ○○○○○○○○○
Difficulty ○○○○○○○○○

Highlights

Notes

Moel-ddu

Height (m): 553m
OS Grid Reference: SH5796244210

Date	Parking ★★★★	Map Ref: 90
Ascent Start Time		Trig Time
Descent Start Time		Finish Time
Ascent Duration	Descent Duration	Total Time
Total Distance Covered		No. Of Steps
Companions		

Weather

- Enjoyment ○○○○○○○○○○
- Views ○○○○○○○○○○
- Difficulty ○○○○○○○○○○

Highlights

Notes

Moel-y-gest

Height (m): 263m
OS Grid Reference: SH5492438891

Date	Parking ★ ★ ★ ★ ★	Map Ref: /91
Ascent Start Time		Trig Time
Descent Start Time		Finish Time
Ascent Duration	Descent Duration	Total Time
Total Distance Covered		No. Of Steps
Companions		
Weather		

Enjoyment ○○○○○○○○○○
Views ○○○○○○○○○○
Difficulty ○○○○○○○○○○

Highlights

Notes

Moelfre

Height (m): 589m
OS Grid Reference: SH6262024588

Date	Parking ☆☆☆☆☆	Map Ref: /92\
Ascent Start Time		Trig Time
Descent Start Time		Finish Time
Ascent Duration	Descent Duration	Total Time
Total Distance Covered		No. Of Steps
Companions		
Weather		

Enjoyment ○○○○○○○○○○
Views ○○○○○○○○○○
Difficulty ○○○○○○○○○○

Highlights

Notes

Moelwyn Mawr

Height (m): 770m
OS Grid Reference: SH6582244861

Map Ref: 93

Date	Parking ★ ★ ★ ★ ★	
Ascent Start Time		Trig Time
Descent Start Time		Finish Time
Ascent Duration	Descent Duration	Total Time
Total Distance Covered		No. Of Steps
Companions		
Weather		

Enjoyment ○ ○ ○ ○ ○ ○ ○ ○ ○ ○
Views ○ ○ ○ ○ ○ ○ ○ ○ ○ ○
Difficulty ○ ○ ○ ○ ○ ○ ○ ○ ○ ○

Highlights

Notes

Mwdwl-eithin

Height (m): 532m
OS Grid Reference: SH9171054056

| Date | Parking ★★★★★ | Map Ref: 94 |

Ascent Start Time | **Trig Time**

Descent Start Time | **Finish Time**

Ascent Duration | **Descent Duration** | **Total Time**

Total Distance Covered | **No. Of Steps**

Companions

Weather

Enjoyment ○○○○○○○○○○
Views ○○○○○○○○○○
Difficulty ○○○○○○○○○○

Highlights

Notes

Myarth

Height (m): 292m
OS Grid Reference: SO1709820836

Date	Parking ☆☆☆☆☆	Map Ref: /95\
Ascent Start Time		Trig Time
Descent Start Time		Finish Time
Ascent Duration	Descent Duration	Total Time
Total Distance Covered		No. Of Steps
Companions		
Weather		

Enjoyment ○○○○○○○○○○
Views ○○○○○○○○○○
Difficulty ○○○○○○○○○○

Highlights

Notes

Mynydd Allt-y-grug

Height (m): 338.7m
OS Grid Reference: SN7532708134

Date	Parking ★★★★★	Map Ref: /96\

Ascent Start Time	Trig Time

Descent Start Time	Finish Time

Ascent Duration	Descent Duration	Total Time

Total Distance Covered	No. Of Steps

Companions

Weather

Enjoyment ○○○○○○○○○○
Views ○○○○○○○○○○
Difficulty ○○○○○○○○○○

Highlights

Notes

Mynydd Anelog

Height (m): 191.4m
OS Grid Reference: SH1519427218

Date	Parking ★★★★★	Map Ref: /97\

Ascent Start Time | **Trig Time**

Descent Start Time | **Finish Time**

Ascent Duration | **Descent Duration** | **Total Time**

Total Distance Covered | **No. Of Steps**

Companions

Weather

Enjoyment ○○○○○○○○○○
Views ○○○○○○○○○○
Difficulty ○○○○○○○○○○

Highlights

Notes

Mynydd Bodafon (Yr Arwydd)

Height (m): 177.6m
OS Grid Reference: SH4724485418

Date	Parking ★★★★★	Map Ref: 98
Ascent Start Time		Trig Time
Descent Start Time		Finish Time
Ascent Duration	Descent Duration	Total Time
Total Distance Covered		No. Of Steps
Companions		
Weather		

Enjoyment ○○○○○○○○○○
Views ○○○○○○○○○○
Difficulty ○○○○○○○○○○

Highlights

Notes

Mynydd Carn-y-cefn

Height (m): 550m
OS Grid Reference: SO1871908497

| Date | Parking ★★★★★★ | Map Ref: /99 |

Ascent Start Time | **Trig Time**

Descent Start Time | **Finish Time**

Ascent Duration | **Descent Duration** | **Total Time**

Total Distance Covered | **No. Of Steps**

Companions

Weather

Enjoyment ○○○○○○○○○○
Views ○○○○○○○○○○
Difficulty ○○○○○○○○○○

Highlights

Notes

Mynydd Carningli

Height (m): 346m
OS Grid Reference: SN0624037226

Date	Parking ★★★★★	Map Ref: /100\
Ascent Start Time		Trig Time
Descent Start Time		Finish Time
Ascent Duration	Descent Duration	Total Time
Total Distance Covered		No. Of Steps
Companions		

Weather

Enjoment ○ ○ ○ ○ ○ ○ ○ ○ ○ ○
Views   ○ ○ ○ ○ ○ ○ ○ ○ ○ ○
Difficulty ○ ○ ○ ○ ○ ○ ○ ○ ○ ○

Highlights

Notes

Mynydd Cynros

Height (m): 329m
OS Grid Reference: SN6205632685

Date	Parking ★★★★★	Map Ref: /101

Ascent Start Time | **Trig Time**

Descent Start Time | **Finish Time**

Ascent Duration | **Descent Duration** | **Total Time**

Total Distance Covered | **No. Of Steps**

Companions

Weather

Enjoyment ○○○○○○○○○○
Views ○○○○○○○○○○
Difficulty ○○○○○○○○○○

Highlights

Notes

Mynydd Dinas

Height (m): 258.1m
OS Grid Reference: SS7614491530

Date	Parking ★★★★★	Map Ref: /102\

Ascent Start Time		Trig Time	

Descent Start Time		Finish Time	

Ascent Duration	Descent Duration	Total Time

Total Distance Covered		No. Of Steps

Companions

Weather

Enjoyment ○ ○ ○ ○ ○ ○ ○ ○ ○ ○
Views   ○ ○ ○ ○ ○ ○ ○ ○ ○ ○
Difficulty ○ ○ ○ ○ ○ ○ ○ ○ ○ ○

Highlights

Notes

Mynydd Drumau

Height (m): 272m
OS Grid Reference: SN7250100176

Date	Parking ☆☆☆☆☆	Map Ref: /103\

Ascent Start Time — **Trig Time**

Descent Start Time — **Finish Time**

Ascent Duration — **Descent Duration** — **Total Time**

Total Distance Covered — **No. Of Steps**

Companions

Weather

- Enjoyment ○○○○○○○○○○
- Views ○○○○○○○○○○
- Difficulty ○○○○○○○○○○

Highlights

Notes

Mynydd Enlli

Height (m): 167.9m
OS Grid Reference: SH1231221931

Date	Parking ★ ★ ★ ★ ★	Map Ref: /104\
Ascent Start Time		Trig Time
Descent Start Time		Finish Time
Ascent Duration	Descent Duration	Total Time
Total Distance Covered		No. Of Steps
Companions		
Weather		

Enjoyment ○ ○ ○ ○ ○ ○ ○ ○ ○ ○
Views   ○ ○ ○ ○ ○ ○ ○ ○ ○ ○
Difficulty ○ ○ ○ ○ ○ ○ ○ ○ ○ ○

Highlights

Notes

Mynydd Epynt (Mynydd Eppynt) ✓

Height (m): 475.5m
OS Grid Reference: SN9612446429

Date	Parking ★★★★★	Map Ref: /105\
Ascent Start Time		Trig Time
Descent Start Time		Finish Time
Ascent Duration	Descent Duration	Total Time
Total Distance Covered		No. Of Steps
Companions		
Weather		

Enjoyment ○○○○○○○○○○
Views ○○○○○○○○○○
Difficulty ○○○○○○○○○○

Highlights

Notes

Mynydd Llangorse

Height (m): 515m
OS Grid Reference: SO1593626699

Date	Parking ★★★★★	Map Ref: /106\
Ascent Start Time		Trig Time
Descent Start Time		Finish Time
Ascent Duration	Descent Duration	Total Time
Total Distance Covered		No. Of Steps
Companions		

Weather

Enjoyment ○○○○○○○○○○
Views ○○○○○○○○○○
Difficulty ○○○○○○○○○○

Highlights

Notes

Mynydd Llangyndeyrn

Height (m): 263m
OS Grid Reference: SN4823613269

Date	Parking	Map Ref: 107

Ascent Start Time		Trig Time	

Descent Start Time		Finish Time	

Ascent Duration	Descent Duration	Total Time

Total Distance Covered	No. Of Steps

Companions

Weather

Enjoyment ○ ○ ○ ○ ○ ○ ○ ○ ○ ○
Views ○ ○ ○ ○ ○ ○ ○ ○ ○ ○
Difficulty ○ ○ ○ ○ ○ ○ ○ ○ ○ ○

Highlights

Notes

Mynydd Machen

Height (m): 363.2m
OS Grid Reference: ST2238190013

Date	Parking ☆☆☆☆☆	Map Ref: 108
Ascent Start Time		Trig Time
Descent Start Time		Finish Time
Ascent Duration	Descent Duration	Total Time
Total Distance Covered		No. Of Steps
Companions		

Weather

Enjoment ○○○○○○○○○○
Views ○○○○○○○○○○
Difficulty ○○○○○○○○○○

Highlights

Notes

Mynydd Marchywel

Height (m): 418m
OS Grid Reference: SN7681903768

Date	Parking ☆☆☆☆☆	Map Ref: /109\
Ascent Start Time		Trig Time
Descent Start Time		Finish Time
Ascent Duration	Descent Duration	Total Time
Total Distance Covered		No. Of Steps
Companions		
Weather		

Enjoracie ○ ○ ○ ○ ○ ○ ○ ○ ○ ○
Views ○ ○ ○ ○ ○ ○ ○ ○ ○ ○
Difficulty ○ ○ ○ ○ ○ ○ ○ ○ ○ ○

Highlights

Notes

Mynydd Mawr

Height (m): 698m
OS Grid Reference: SH5397254692

Date	Parking ★ ★ ★ ★ ★	Map Ref: 110

Ascent Start Time	Trig Time

Descent Start Time	Finish Time

Ascent Duration	Descent Duration	Total Time

Total Distance Covered	No. Of Steps

Companions

Weather

- Enjoyment ○ ○ ○ ○ ○ ○ ○ ○ ○ ○
- Views ○ ○ ○ ○ ○ ○ ○ ○ ○ ○
- Difficulty ○ ○ ○ ○ ○ ○ ○ ○ ○ ○

Highlights

Notes

Mynydd Nodol

Height (m): 539m
OS Grid Reference: SH8651239343

Date	Parking ☆☆☆☆☆	Map Ref: /111\
Ascent Start Time		Trig Time
Descent Start Time		Finish Time
Ascent Duration	Descent Duration	Total Time
Total Distance Covered		No. Of Steps

Companions

Weather

Enjoment ○○○○○○○○○○
Views ○○○○○○○○○○
Difficulty ○○○○○○○○○○

Highlights

Notes

Mynydd Rhiw

Height (m): 304m
OS Grid Reference: SH2284629388

Date	Parking ★★★★★	Map Ref: 112
Ascent Start Time		Trig Time
Descent Start Time		Finish Time
Ascent Duration	Descent Duration	Total Time
Total Distance Covered		No. Of Steps
Companions		

Weather

Enjoyment ○○○○○○○○○○
Views ○○○○○○○○○○
Difficulty ○○○○○○○○○○

Highlights

Notes

Mynydd Rhyd Ddu

Height (m): 389m
OS Grid Reference: SJ0545547743

Date	Parking ★★★★★	Map Ref: /113\
Ascent Start Time		Trig Time
Descent Start Time		Finish Time
Ascent Duration	Descent Duration	Total Time
Total Distance Covered		No. Of Steps
Companions		
Weather		

Enjoyment ○○○○○○○○○○
Views ○○○○○○○○○○
Difficulty ○○○○○○○○○○

Highlights

Notes

Mynydd Sylen

Height (m): 284m
OS Grid Reference: SN5153308009

Date	Parking ★★★★★	Map Ref: 114

Ascent Start Time	Trig Time

Descent Start Time	Finish Time

Ascent Duration	Descent Duration	Total Time

Total Distance Covered	No. Of Steps

Companions

Weather

Enjoyment ○ ○ ○ ○ ○ ○ ○ ○ ○ ○
Views ○ ○ ○ ○ ○ ○ ○ ○ ○ ○
Difficulty ○ ○ ○ ○ ○ ○ ○ ○ ○ ○

Highlights

Notes

Mynydd Troed

Height (m): 609m
OS Grid Reference: SO1656629232

Date	Parking	Map Ref: /115\
Ascent Start Time		Trig Time
Descent Start Time		Finish Time
Ascent Duration	Descent Duration	Total Time
Total Distance Covered		No. Of Steps
Companions		

Weather

Enjoyment ○○○○○○○○○○
Views ○○○○○○○○○○
Difficulty ○○○○○○○○○○

Highlights

Notes

Mynydd Twyn-glas

Height (m): 472m
OS Grid Reference: ST2599997845

Date	Parking ★★★★★	Map Ref: 116

Ascent Start Time	Trig Time

Descent Start Time	Finish Time

Ascent Duration	Descent Duration	Total Time

Total Distance Covered	No. Of Steps

Companions

Weather

Enjoyment ○○○○○○○○○○
Views ○○○○○○○○○○
Difficulty ○○○○○○○○○○

Highlights

Notes

Mynydd Uchaf

Height (m): 357m
OS Grid Reference: SN7156410309

Date	Parking ★★★★★	Map Ref: /117\
Ascent Start Time		Trig Time
Descent Start Time		Finish Time
Ascent Duration	Descent Duration	Total Time
Total Distance Covered		No. Of Steps
Companions		
Weather		

Enjoment ○○○○○○○○○○
Views ○○○○○○○○○○
Difficulty ○○○○○○○○○○

Highlights

Notes

Mynydd y Betws

Height (m): 373.1m
OS Grid Reference: SN6647009482

Date	Parking ★★★★★	Map Ref: 118
Ascent Start Time		Trig Time
Descent Start Time		Finish Time
Ascent Duration	Descent Duration	Total Time
Total Distance Covered		No. Of Steps
Companions		
Weather		

Enjoyment ○ ○ ○ ○ ○ ○ ○ ○ ○ ○
Views   ○ ○ ○ ○ ○ ○ ○ ○ ○ ○
Difficulty ○ ○ ○ ○ ○ ○ ○ ○ ○ ○

Highlights

Notes

Mynydd y Cwm (Coed Cwm)

Height (m): 304.8m
OS Grid Reference: SJ0730576732

Date	Parking ☆☆☆☆☆	Map Ref: /119\
Ascent Start Time		Trig Time
Descent Start Time		Finish Time
Ascent Duration	Descent Duration	Total Time
Total Distance Covered		No. Of Steps
Companions		
Weather		

Enjoyment ○○○○○○○○○○
Views ○○○○○○○○○○
Difficulty ○○○○○○○○○○

Highlights

Notes

Mynydd y Glyn

Height (m): 377m
OS Grid Reference: ST0319189642

Date	Parking ★★★★★	Map Ref: /120\

Ascent Start Time	Trig Time

Descent Start Time	Finish Time

Ascent Duration	Descent Duration	Total Time

Total Distance Covered	No. Of Steps

Companions

Weather

Enjoyment ○○○○○○○○○○
Views ○○○○○○○○○○
Difficulty ○○○○○○○○○○

Highlights

Notes

Mynydd y Lan

Height (m): 381.3m
OS Grid Reference: ST2090392340

Date	Parking ★★★★★	Map Ref: 121

Ascent Start Time | **Trig Time**

Descent Start Time | **Finish Time**

Ascent Duration | **Descent Duration** | **Total Time**

Total Distance Covered | **No. Of Steps**

Companions

Weather

Enjoyment ○○○○○○○○○
Views ○○○○○○○○○
Difficulty ○○○○○○○○○

Highlights

Notes

Mynydd-y-briw

Height (m): 341m
OS Grid Reference: SJ1740226070

Date	Parking ★★★★★	Map Ref: 122

Ascent Start Time		Trig Time	
Descent Start Time		Finish Time	
Ascent Duration	Descent Duration		Total Time
Total Distance Covered		No. Of Steps	
Companions			

Weather

Enjoyment ○○○○○○○○○○
Views ○○○○○○○○○○
Difficulty ○○○○○○○○○○

Highlights

Notes

Pegwn Mawr

Height (m): 586m
OS Grid Reference: SO0239281242

Date	Parking ★★★★★	Map Ref: /123\
Ascent Start Time		Trig Time
Descent Start Time		Finish Time
Ascent Duration	Descent Duration	Total Time
Total Distance Covered		No. Of Steps
Companions		
Weather		

Enjoment ○○○○○○○○○○
Views ○○○○○○○○○○
Difficulty ○○○○○○○○○○

Highlights

Notes

Pen Llithrig y Wrach

Height (m): 798.6m
OS Grid Reference: SH7162262290

Date	Parking ★★★★★	Map Ref: 124
Ascent Start Time		Trig Time
Descent Start Time		Finish Time
Ascent Duration	Descent Duration	Total Time
Total Distance Covered		No. Of Steps
Companions		

Weather

Enjoyment ○○○○○○○○○○
Views ○○○○○○○○○○
Difficulty ○○○○○○○○○○

Highlights

Notes

Pen y Fan

Height (m): 886m
OS Grid Reference: SO0120821583

Date	Parking ☆☆☆☆☆	Map Ref: /125\
Ascent Start Time		Trig Time
Descent Start Time		Finish Time
Ascent Duration	Descent Duration	Total Time
Total Distance Covered		No. Of Steps
Companions		
Weather		

Enjoyment ○○○○○○○○○○
Views ○○○○○○○○○○
Difficulty ○○○○○○○○○○

Highlights

Notes

Pen y Garn

Height (m): 611m
OS Grid Reference: SN7985477143

Date	Parking ★★★★★	Map Ref: 126
Ascent Start Time		Trig Time
Descent Start Time		Finish Time
Ascent Duration	Descent Duration	Total Time
Total Distance Covered		No. Of Steps
Companions		

Weather

Enjoreent ○○○○○○○○○○
Views ○○○○○○○○○○
Difficulty ○○○○○○○○○○

Highlights

Notes

Pen y Garn-goch

Height (m): 487m
OS Grid Reference: SN8848250281

Date	Parking	Map Ref: /127

Ascent Start Time	Trig Time

Descent Start Time	Finish Time

Ascent Duration	Descent Duration	Total Time

Total Distance Covered	No. Of Steps

Companions

Weather

- Enjoyment ○ ○ ○ ○ ○ ○ ○ ○ ○ ○
- Views ○ ○ ○ ○ ○ ○ ○ ○ ○ ○
- Difficulty ○ ○ ○ ○ ○ ○ ○ ○ ○ ○

Highlights

Notes

Pen-crug-melyn

Height (m): 326m
OS Grid Reference: SN5027128503

Date	Parking ★★★★★	Map Ref: /128\
Ascent Start Time		Trig Time
Descent Start Time		Finish Time
Ascent Duration	Descent Duration	Total Time
Total Distance Covered		No. Of Steps
Companions		

Weather

Enjoke ○○○○○○○○○○
Views ○○○○○○○○○○
Difficulty ○○○○○○○○○○

Highlights

Notes

Penycloddiau

Height (m): 439.5m
OS Grid Reference: SJ1271567889

Date	Parking ☆☆☆☆☆	Map Ref: /129\
Ascent Start Time		Trig Time
Descent Start Time		Finish Time
Ascent Duration	Descent Duration	Total Time
Total Distance Covered		No. Of Steps
Companions		
Weather		

Enjoyment ○ ○ ○ ○ ○ ○ ○ ○
Views ○ ○ ○ ○ ○ ○ ○ ○
Difficulty ○ ○ ○ ○ ○ ○ ○ ○

Highlights

Notes

Pumlumon Fawr (Plynlimon)

Height (m): 752m
OS Grid Reference: SN7896986941

Date	Parking ★★★★★	Map Ref: /130\
Ascent Start Time		Trig Time
Descent Start Time		Finish Time
Ascent Duration	Descent Duration	Total Time
Total Distance Covered		No. Of Steps
Companions		

Weather

Enjoure ○○○○○○○○○○
Views ○○○○○○○○○○
Difficulty ○○○○○○○○○○

Highlights

Notes

Rhialgwm

Height (m): 540m
OS Grid Reference: SJ0550121175

Date	Parking ★★★★★	Map Ref: /131\
Ascent Start Time		Trig Time
Descent Start Time		Finish Time
Ascent Duration	Descent Duration	Total Time
Total Distance Covered		No. Of Steps
Companions		
Weather		

Enjoyment ○○○○○○○○○○
Views ○○○○○○○○○○
Difficulty ○○○○○○○○○○

Highlights

Notes

Rhinog Fawr

Height (m): 720m
OS Grid Reference: SH6569729008

Date	Parking ★★★★★	Map Ref: /132\
Ascent Start Time		Trig Time
Descent Start Time		Finish Time
Ascent Duration	Descent Duration	Total Time
Total Distance Covered		No. Of Steps
Companions		
Weather		

Enjoyment ○○○○○○○○○○
Views ○○○○○○○○○○
Difficulty ○○○○○○○○○○

Highlights

Notes

Rhiw Gwraidd

Height (m): 442m
OS Grid Reference: SO0160863432

Date	Parking ☆☆☆☆☆	Map Ref: /133\
Ascent Start Time		Trig Time
Descent Start Time		Finish Time
Ascent Duration	Descent Duration	Total Time
Total Distance Covered		No. Of Steps
Companions		
Weather		

Enjoyment ○ ○ ○ ○ ○ ○ ○ ○ ○ ○
Views ○ ○ ○ ○ ○ ○ ○ ○ ○ ○
Difficulty ○ ○ ○ ○ ○ ○ ○ ○ ○ ○

Highlights

Notes

Rhinog Fach

Height (m): 712m
OS Grid Reference: SH6648327025

Date	Parking ★★★★★	Map Ref: /134\
Ascent Start Time		Trig Time
Descent Start Time		Finish Time
Ascent Duration	Descent Duration	Total Time
Total Distance Covered		No. Of Steps
Companions		
Weather		

Enjoyment ○ ○ ○ ○ ○ ○ ○ ○ ○ ○
Views ○ ○ ○ ○ ○ ○ ○ ○ ○ ○
Difficulty ○ ○ ○ ○ ○ ○ ○ ○ ○ ○

Highlights

Notes

Rhobell Fawr

Height (m): 734m
OS Grid Reference: SH7868025664

Date	Parking	Map Ref: /135
Ascent Start Time	Trig Time	
Descent Start Time	Finish Time	
Ascent Duration	Descent Duration	Total Time
Total Distance Covered		No. Of Steps
Companions		

Weather

Enjoyment ○○○○○○○○○○
Views ○○○○○○○○○○
Difficulty ○○○○○○○○○○

Highlights

Notes

Rhos Ymryson

Height (m): 327m
OS Grid Reference: SN4603550012

Date	Parking ★ ★ ★ ★ ★	Map Ref: 136
Ascent Start Time		Trig Time
Descent Start Time		Finish Time
Ascent Duration	Descent Duration	Total Time
Total Distance Covered		No. Of Steps
Companions		

Weather

Enjoure ○ ○ ○ ○ ○ ○ ○ ○ ○ ○
Views ○ ○ ○ ○ ○ ○ ○ ○ ○ ○
Difficulty ○ ○ ○ ○ ○ ○ ○ ○ ○ ○

Highlights

Notes

Snowdon - Yr Wyddfa

Height (m): 1085m
OS Grid Reference: SH6098654376

Date	Parking ☆☆☆☆☆	Map Ref: 137

Ascent Start Time | **Trig Time**

Descent Start Time | **Finish Time**

Ascent Duration | **Descent Duration** | **Total Time**

Total Distance Covered | **No. Of Steps**

Companions

Weather

Enjoyment ○○○○○○○○○○
Views ○○○○○○○○○○
Difficulty ○○○○○○○○○○

Highlights

Notes

Stingwern Hill

Height (m): 358m
OS Grid Reference: SJ1328501455

Date	Parking ★★★★★	Map Ref: /138\

Ascent Start Time	Trig Time

Descent Start Time	Finish Time

Ascent Duration	Descent Duration	Total Time

Total Distance Covered	No. Of Steps

Companions

Weather

Enjoyment ○ ○ ○ ○ ○ ○ ○ ○ ○ ○
Views ○ ○ ○ ○ ○ ○ ○ ○ ○ ○
Difficulty ○ ○ ○ ○ ○ ○ ○ ○ ○ ○

Highlights

Notes

Sugar Loaf

Height (m): 596m
OS Grid Reference: SO2725118765

Date	Parking	Map Ref: /139
Ascent Start Time		Trig Time
Descent Start Time		Finish Time
Ascent Duration	Descent Duration	Total Time
Total Distance Covered		No. Of Steps
Companions		
Weather		

Enjoment ○ ○ ○ ○ ○ ○ ○ ○ ○ ○
Views ○ ○ ○ ○ ○ ○ ○ ○ ○ ○
Difficulty ○ ○ ○ ○ ○ ○ ○ ○ ○ ○

Highlights

Notes

Tal y Fan

Height (m): 610m
OS Grid Reference: SH7293672648

Date	Parking ★★★★★	Map Ref: 140

Ascent Start Time	Trig Time

Descent Start Time	Finish Time

Ascent Duration	Descent Duration	Total Time

Total Distance Covered	No. Of Steps

Companions

Weather

Enjoyment ◯◯◯◯◯◯◯◯◯◯
Views ◯◯◯◯◯◯◯◯◯◯
Difficulty ◯◯◯◯◯◯◯◯◯◯

Highlights

Notes

Tarren y Gesail

Height (m): 667m
OS Grid Reference: SH7105005890

Date	Parking	Map Ref: 141

Ascent Start Time — **Trig Time**

Descent Start Time — **Finish Time**

Ascent Duration — **Descent Duration** — **Total Time**

Total Distance Covered — **No. Of Steps**

Companions

Weather

- Enjoyment ◯◯◯◯◯◯◯◯◯◯
- Views ◯◯◯◯◯◯◯◯◯◯
- Difficulty ◯◯◯◯◯◯◯◯◯◯

Highlights

Notes

Tarrenhendre

Height (m): 634m
OS Grid Reference: SH6828104152

Date	Parking ★★★★★	Map Ref: /142\

Ascent Start Time	Trig Time

Descent Start Time	Finish Time

Ascent Duration	Descent Duration	Total Time

Total Distance Covered	No. Of Steps

Companions

Weather

Enjoyment ○○○○○○○○○○
Views ○○○○○○○○○○
Difficulty ○○○○○○○○○○

Highlights

Notes

The Begwns

Height (m): 415m
OS Grid Reference: SO1550044409

Date	Parking ☆☆☆☆☆	Map Ref: 143
Ascent Start Time		Trig Time
Descent Start Time		Finish Time
Ascent Duration	Descent Duration	Total Time
Total Distance Covered		No. Of Steps
Companions		
Weather		

Enjoyment ○○○○○○○○○○
Views ○○○○○○○○○○
Difficulty ○○○○○○○○○○

Highlights

Notes

Tor y Foel

Height (m): 551m
OS Grid Reference: SO1145619493

Date	Parking ☆☆☆☆☆	Map Ref: 144
Ascent Start Time		Trig Time
Descent Start Time		Finish Time
Ascent Duration	Descent Duration	Total Time
Total Distance Covered		No. Of Steps
Companions		

Weather

Enjoyment ○○○○○○○○○○
Views ○○○○○○○○○○
Difficulty ○○○○○○○○○○

Highlights

Notes

Trichrug

Height (m): 415m
OS Grid Reference: SN6989022923

Date	Parking ☆☆☆☆☆	Map Ref: 145
Ascent Start Time		Trig Time
Descent Start Time		Finish Time
Ascent Duration	Descent Duration	Total Time
Total Distance Covered		No. Of Steps
Companions		
Weather		

Enjoint ○○○○○○○○○○
Views ○○○○○○○○○○
Difficulty ○○○○○○○○○○

Highlights

Notes

Trum y Ddysgl

Height (m): 709m
OS Grid Reference: SH5448451643

Date	Parking ★★★★★	Map Ref: /146\
Ascent Start Time		Trig Time
Descent Start Time		Finish Time
Ascent Duration	Descent Duration	Total Time
Total Distance Covered		No. Of Steps

Companions

Weather

Enjoyment ○○○○○○○○○○
Views ○○○○○○○○○○
Difficulty ○○○○○○○○○○

Highlights

Notes

Tryfan

Height (m): 917.5m
OS Grid Reference: SH6640559387

Date	Parking ☆☆☆☆☆	Map Ref: /147\
Ascent Start Time		Trig Time
Descent Start Time		Finish Time
Ascent Duration	Descent Duration	Total Time
Total Distance Covered		No. Of Steps
Companions		
Weather		

Enjoyment ○○○○○○○○○○
Views ○○○○○○○○○○
Difficulty ○○○○○○○○○○

Highlights

Notes

Upper Park

Height (m): 352m
OS Grid Reference: SJ1897505271

Date	Parking ☆☆☆☆☆	Map Ref: /148\
Ascent Start Time		Trig Time
Descent Start Time		Finish Time
Ascent Duration	Descent Duration	Total Time
Total Distance Covered		No. Of Steps
Companions		
Weather		

Enjoyment ○○○○○○○○○○
Views ○○○○○○○○○○
Difficulty ○○○○○○○○○○

Highlights

Notes

Waun Fach

Height (m): 811m
OS Grid Reference: SO2155129984

Date	Parking ☆☆☆☆☆	Map Ref: /149
Ascent Start Time		Trig Time
Descent Start Time		Finish Time
Ascent Duration	Descent Duration	Total Time
Total Distance Covered		No. Of Steps
Companions		
Weather		

Enjoyment ○○○○○○○○○○
Views ○○○○○○○○○○
Difficulty ○○○○○○○○○○

Highlights

Notes

Waun Rydd

Height (m): 769.2m
OS Grid Reference: SO0621220645

Date	Parking ★★★★★	Map Ref: /150\
Ascent Start Time		Trig Time
Descent Start Time		Finish Time
Ascent Duration	Descent Duration	Total Time
Total Distance Covered		No. Of Steps
Companions		
Weather		

Enjoyment ○○○○○○○○○○
Views ○○○○○○○○○○
Difficulty ○○○○○○○○○○

Highlights

Notes

Wentwood

Height (m): 309.1m
OS Grid Reference: ST4113194309

Date	Parking	Map Ref: 151

Ascent Start Time | **Trig Time**

Descent Start Time | **Finish Time**

Ascent Duration | **Descent Duration** | **Total Time**

Total Distance Covered | **No. Of Steps**

Companions

Weather

- Enjoyment ○○○○○○○○○○
- Views ○○○○○○○○○○
- Difficulty ○○○○○○○○○○

Highlights

Notes

Y Garn

Height (m): 629m
OS Grid Reference: SH7027323026

Date	Parking ★★★★★	Map Ref: /152\
Ascent Start Time		Trig Time
Descent Start Time		Finish Time
Ascent Duration	Descent Duration	Total Time
Total Distance Covered		No. Of Steps
Companions		

Weather

Enjoyment ○○○○○○○○○○
Views ○○○○○○○○○○
Difficulty ○○○○○○○○○○

Highlights

Notes

Y Garn

Height (m): 947m
OS Grid Reference: SH6308959569

Date	Parking ☆☆☆☆☆	Map Ref: 153
Ascent Start Time		Trig Time
Descent Start Time		Finish Time
Ascent Duration	Descent Duration	Total Time
Total Distance Covered		No. Of Steps
Companions		
Weather		

Enjoyment ○○○○○○○○○○
Views ○○○○○○○○○○
Difficulty ○○○○○○○○○○

Highlights

Notes

Y Golfa

Height (m): 341.4m
OS Grid Reference: SJ1825007088

Date	Parking ★★★★★	Map Ref: /154\
Ascent Start Time		Trig Time
Descent Start Time		Finish Time
Ascent Duration	Descent Duration	Total Time
Total Distance Covered		No. Of Steps
Companions		
Weather		

Enjoyment ○ ○ ○ ○ ○ ○ ○ ○ ○ ○
Views ○ ○ ○ ○ ○ ○ ○ ○ ○ ○
Difficulty ○ ○ ○ ○ ○ ○ ○ ○ ○ ○

Highlights

Notes

Y Llethr

Height (m): 756m
OS Grid Reference: SH6613425773

Date	Parking ☆☆☆☆☆	Map Ref: /155\
Ascent Start Time		Trig Time
Descent Start Time		Finish Time
Ascent Duration	Descent Duration	Total Time
Total Distance Covered		No. Of Steps
Companions		
Weather		

Enjoyment ○○○○○○○○○○
Views ○○○○○○○○○○
Difficulty ○○○○○○○○○○

Highlights

Notes

Y Lliwedd

Height (m): 898m
OS Grid Reference: SH6224253336

Date	Parking ★★★★★	Map Ref: 156

Ascent Start Time	Trig Time

Descent Start Time	Finish Time

Ascent Duration	Descent Duration	Total Time

Total Distance Covered	No. Of Steps

Companions

Weather

Enjoyment ○○○○○○○○○○
Views ○○○○○○○○○○
Difficulty ○○○○○○○○○○

Highlights

Notes

Yr Aran

Height (m): 747.2m
OS Grid Reference: SH6043751528

Date	Parking	Map Ref: 157

Ascent Start Time		Trig Time	
Descent Start Time		Finish Time	
Ascent Duration	Descent Duration		Total Time
Total Distance Covered		No. Of Steps	
Companions			

Weather

Enjoyment ○ ○ ○ ○ ○ ○ ○ ○ ○ ○
Views ○ ○ ○ ○ ○ ○ ○ ○ ○ ○
Difficulty ○ ○ ○ ○ ○ ○ ○ ○ ○ ○

Highlights

Notes

Yr Eifl

Height (m): 560.7m
OS Grid Reference: SH3649144744

Date	Parking ★★★★★	Map Ref: /158\
Ascent Start Time		Trig Time
Descent Start Time		Finish Time
Ascent Duration	Descent Duration	Total Time
Total Distance Covered		No. Of Steps
Companions		

Weather

Enjoyment ○○○○○○○○○○
Views ○○○○○○○○○○
Difficulty ○○○○○○○○○○

Highlights

Notes

Ysgyryd Fawr

Height (m): 486m
OS Grid Reference: SO3311618278

Date	Parking ☆☆☆☆☆	Map Ref: /159\
Ascent Start Time		Trig Time
Descent Start Time		Finish Time
Ascent Duration	Descent Duration	Total Time
Total Distance Covered		No. Of Steps
Companions		
Weather		

Enjoyment ○○○○○○○○○○
Views ○○○○○○○○○○
Difficulty ○○○○○○○○○○

Highlights

Notes

Ready for your next adventure?

Keeping a log book is a fantastic way of recording your memories - and we have published a number of adventure log books available on Amazon. Simply scan the QR code to find out more!

Printed in Great Britain
by Amazon